What Is Modern Sculpture?

Robert Goldwater

The Museum of Modern Art, New York

Distributed by New York Graphic Society Ltd., Greenwich, Connecticut

Photograph Credits

Photographs not credited below were obtained from The Museum of Modern Art.

Brassaï, Paris, 25; Rudolph Burckhardt, New York, 87, 109, 110; Geoffrey Clements, New York, 16 left, 80, 88; Cranbrook Academy of Art, Bloomfield Hills, Mich., 40; Comet, Zurich, 100; Photo Service T.I.P. Daniel, Liège, 71; Walter Dräyer, Zurich, 54 left; David Farrell, London, 113; Thomas Feist, New York (Courtesy Albert Loeb and Krugier Gallery, New York), 86; Stephen Frisch, Sausalito, Calif., 98; Courtesy Roberta Gonzalez, 74; Sherwin Greenberg Studio, Inc., Buffalo, 85; Sherwin Greenberg, McGranahan & May, Inc., Buffalo, 106; Courtesy David Hare, New York, 54 right; W. Hartmann, Ottawa, 19; John Hedgecoe, London, 13; The Joseph H. Hirschhorn Collection, New York, 24 right, 61; Peter Juley & Son, New York, 115; Kunsthaus, Zurich, 57; Kim Lim (Courtesy Kasmin Limited, London), 105; Courtesy Victor A. Lundy, New York, 140; Man Ray, 52; L. Marinoff, New York, 120; Robert E. Mates, New York, 99; James Mathews, New York, 35, 103, 112; Herbert Matter, New York, 50, 70, 75; Metropolitan Museum of Art, New York, 27 left, 30; Courtesy Mrs. Sibyl Moholy-Nagy, New York, 68; Henry Moore, 126; Peter Moore, New York, 96; André Morain, Paris (Courtesy Breteau Gallery, Paris), 90; Musée Bourdelle, Paris, 38; Musée Rodin, Meudon, 132; O. E. Nelson, New York, 29, 47; Rolf Petersen, New York, 14, 51, 104, 108; Philadelphia Museum of Art, 41, 94; Eric Pollitzer, Garden City Park, N.Y., 119; Rheinisches Bildarchiv, Kölnisches Stadtmuseum, Germany, 125; Cervin Robinson, New York, 137; Ernst Scheidegger, Zurich, 11; Service de documentation photographique, Union de Musées nationaux, Versailles, 58; Courtesy Michel Seuphor, Paris, 128; David Smith (Courtesy Edward Fry, New York), 84; The Solomon R. Guggenheim Museum, New York, 56, 66; Ezra Stoller Associates, Rye, N.Y., 130, 138, 139; Adolph Studly, New York, 21; Soichi Sunami, New York, 10, 15, 16 right, 17, 18, 23, 28, 31, 36, 37, 39, 43, 44, 45, 46, 49, 55, 60 bottom, 60 top, 62, 67, 76, 78, 79, 81, 83, 93, 95, 97, 114, 116, 117, 118, 121, 122, 124; Steven Trefonides, Boston, 26; Eduard Trier, Düsseldorf, 129; Charles Uht, New York, 111; Malcolm Varon, New York, 123; Courtesy Alex Vömel, Düsseldorf, 27 right; John Webb, London, 53, 73; A. J. Wyatt, Philadelphia, 22; Yale University Art Gallery, New Haven, Conn., 65.

© 1969, The Museum of Modern Art
11 West 53 Street, New York, New York 10019
Library of Congress Catalogue Card
   Number 76–86420
Designed by Joseph Bourke Del Valle
Type set by Dayton Typographic Service,
   Dayton, Ohio
Printed by Rapoport Printing Corp., New York
Bound by Sendor Bindery, Inc., New York
Cover photograph by Malcolm Varon

Acknowledgments

The first suggestion of my writing this book came from Monroe Wheeler, and I wish to thank him for our initial discussions and his subsequent interest. William Rubin, Bates Lowry, and Irene Gordon read a draft of the text and made pertinent criticisms and suggestions. Harriet Schoenholz has been both precise and sympathetic in her editing of the text, and she and Anne Hecht have been resourceful in their pursuit of photographs. Nadia Hermos gathered the material for the biographies. I am grateful to Joseph Del Valle whose design has given a sensitive structure to the fundamentally visual intention of this book. Jack Doenias has supervised its production. I am especially indebted to Helen Franc who has joined criticism and enthusiasm in a professional and friendly concern. The generous hospitality of Aimone Negretto Cambiaso during a Lucchese summer allowed me to finish the writing and revision of the text. Finally, I should like to acknowledge the indirect contribution of Alfred H. Barr, Jr., whose *What Is Modern Painting?*, the first of this series, is a model of clarity and conciseness.

R. G.

For René d'Harnoncourt

Contents

Introduction

This book is an introduction to modern sculpture. It illustrates the sculpture of this century through selected examples, and briefly explains their formal character and the intentions that prompted their creation. Therefore its range is broad in both time and style. It spans some seventy-five years—from just before 1900 to the present; and it includes many kinds of sculpture, since such variety is characteristic of the art of our time.

The following pages are, however, not a history, with all that this would imply of sources, influences, development, and biographical detail. The emphasis has rather been upon a more direct apprehension and appreciation of a representative selection of individual works of art, and on their understanding and enjoyment when they are encountered as they were conceived—for themselves. As far as is possible within the format of a book, the works included here have been arranged as though in an exhibition; the grouping is such that related works can be seen together, and the texts are always close to the illustrations. The restricted format of this volume has imposed severe limitations and forced the omission of many works, and the works of many other artists, which, given more space, would have been included. The quality of modern sculpture is not confined to those given here.

The book's general structure is more symmetrical than sequential. The opening and closing sections of the text are nonhistorical and illustrate contrasting interpretations of similar themes or problems. In the central section, the tendencies of modern sculpture have been grouped by style, an arrangement necessarily entailing considerations of period; even here, however, affinities of form and intention have been given precedence over the details of historical development.

A word about the twelve divisions of the middle section—and their titles—is in order. Classification of this kind is always partially unreal and partially unfair: unreal because it is an abstraction from individual, concrete works; unfair because it calls undue attention to a least common denominator and ignores the specific, subtle factors which constitute character and quality. But such classification is also both real and useful: real because artists do share methods, goals, and philosophies,

belong to groups, are friends, and even draw up programs; useful because the names we give summon up the whole rich fabric of milieu and idea in which the artist worked and within which he viewed his own creation. Insofar as this context must be recalled, history cannot be avoided.

The classifying names employed here are of various origins and have varying implications and latitude. Thus impressionism and symbolism have been used to suggest that the work of a few sculptors, who were never members of any group, had certain broad parallels with the painting of their time. Cubism, futurism, dada, and surrealism, on the other hand, are all terms the artists themselves used, and (cubism excepted) describe an initially cohesive group and program. But while the first cubist and futurist sculpture followed in the immediate wake of the painting, adapting its aims to sculpture, the first dada and surrealist sculptors contributed from the start to a common formulation of artistic goals. And the manifesto of constructivism was drawn up solely by sculptors.

These groups—cubists, futurists, dadaists, surrealists, constructivists—were all part of the beginnings of modern art; they belonged to specific times and places. Only later did their ideas spread, to become underlying currents in a broadening, changing stream.

Reflecting this change, the terms biomorphism, space drawing, expressionist constructivism, and assemblage are of a different, and more artificial, sort. They have been coined by critics to express relationships of a much more generalized and widespread kind, often among artists of different generations and countries who have had no direct contact with one another. They are meant to suggest perceived similarities among works by artists who, being heirs to the whole heritage of modern art, may or may not be conscious of their

sources and affinities. They indicate the existence of the contemporaneous international tendencies that have characterized the growth and diffusion of modern art during the last three decades.

Throughout the nineteenth century there was a sharply drawn line between painting and sculpture. With rare exceptions (Géricault, Degas, Gauguin) painters did not try their hand at sculpture. Since 1900 this has changed radically. Some of the greatest artists of this century, while devoting most of their energies to painting, have periodically immersed themselves in sculpture, creating work important for itself and for its influence upon other sculptors. Matisse, Picasso, Miró, and Ernst have been seminal figures for both painting and sculpture. The same is true of Giacometti, who turned to painting only toward the end of his life.

This bursting of limits was more than the result of individual genius—although it was that too. Quite generally, the former demarcations between the arts, and between kinds within each of the arts, no longer held good. Distinctions that used to be made between relief and sculpture in the round, between carving and modeling and what was proper to each; ideas about "truth to materials" and the qualities inherent in and exclusive to bronze casting, wood cutting and stone carving; fixed notions about the impropriety of mixing materials or of using color as an essential ingredient of sculpture to heighten or modify its formal impact—all these were discarded. An even more basic result of the new attitudes was to remove the rigid separations between painting and sculpture and between sculpture and the object, and, about 1920 and again more recently, to permit certain kinds of sculpture to move toward architecture in its handling of monumental space and abstract form.

One accompaniment of this new freedom

has been the investigation and use of new materials and techniques, whose possibilities have in their turn affected the character of modern sculpture. Sculptors have of course continued to employ the traditional materials of their craft, but they have also felt free to work in any other available materials. As early as 1915, under the initial influence of collage, artists in France, Italy, Germany, and Russia had begun not only to employ such unconventional substances as tin, iron, cloth, glass, and celluloid, but to mix them (and wood and plaster as well) in the same work and to apply color where it seemed appropriate. By 1920 the constructivists emphasized glass and plastics for their translucent qualities, and about 1930 González and Picasso were employing iron for large-scale work. Since then steel, aluminum, copper, metal wire, plywood and pressed wood, rubber in many forms, and all the more recent varieties of plastics have entered the sculptural vocabulary, and the handling of these new materials naturally has called for new techniques. But it is characteristic that, new or traditional, these skills were not valued for their own sakes, or, as in many forms of assemblage, were deliberately minimized. Means and materials were only justified by the success of the work they served.

Modern technology has in this way been a factor in the development of modern sculpture. But its determining importance should not be overestimated. It made possible, and sometimes it suggested, new kinds of sculpture. Other than that, technology has been one part of a larger context, all of whose elements —physical, social, intellectual, psychological, and spiritual—were new and constantly changing. It is the modern sculptor's responses —as a sculptor—to this total environment, the renewed ordering created by his artistic imagination (entailing a repeated disordering of the conventional and the accepted), the variety of his solutions as an artist giving meaning to three-dimensional form, that are the subject of this book.

The Human Figure

From prehistoric times, sculptors have modeled and chiseled the human figure. They have portrayed gods and heroes of the past and made portraits of contemporary men. Although they were interested in the beauty and expressiveness of the human form for its own sake, they used that form chiefly as a way of making its subject real, of communicating the ideas and associations connected with it. Thus the sculptor employed the human figure to give tangible form to concepts and symbols already familiar to his audience. The shape and the substance he gave these familiar symbols were largely traditional, and easily recognizable; in turn, the particular way he rendered them, which came from his needs and the needs of his time, influenced the way in which religious and civic figures were conceived.

The modern sculptor has used the human figure in a different fashion; his problem has been both more and less difficult. Like the painter, he usually has worked for himself, rather than for a private or public patron, and his work has answered his personal demands first and found a public response only after it has been completed. Its meaning must therefore be discovered less in the subject matter than in the character and the manner—the style—of the work itself.

Despiau's *Assia* is a traditional nude. Although it is the figure of a young woman, it is not especially idealized or impersonal; neither, despite its title, is it altogether a portrait. Its pose is quiet, the weight of the body resting on one leg, with feet together and arms at rest; but through the placing of the hands and the movement of the head, Despiau has emphasized the casual over the monumental. He has also balanced the firmness and weight of the body, and its compactness, against the

10

play of light on the skin and hair, and especially on the face, which is felt without any individual expression. The turned head, with its glance away from the spectator, further reduces any sense of personality and also suggests the surrounding space implied by the reflections from the body. It is a figure at once typical and casual, generalized and individual, and in all these calculated balances embodies at least one kind of naturalism.

In contrast, Giacometti's *Man Pointing* tends toward expressionism. There are obvious exaggerations in the extreme slenderness, the sticklike legs, the reduced head, and the arms so reduced that they seem like a flow of energy culminating in the enormous, pointing finger. Like the face's energetic profile and directed glance (very different from the subdued withdrawal of the Despiau), the finger leads toward an infinite space. As Giacometti has explained, he sees the surrounding atmosphere eating away at the figure's mass, its irregular, lumpy surface drawing light into dark, absorbing hollows, leaving only its bare emaciation. Naturalistic proportions are reduced, transformed, concentrated in the single gesture that seems to point beyond its own isolation.

opposite
Charles Despiau
Assia. 1938

left
Alberto Giacometti
Man Pointing. 1947

left
Julio González
The Montserrat. 1936–37

opposite
Pablo Picasso
Man with Sheep. 1944

The Montserrat is the name of Catalonia's holy mountain; it is also a name common among its women. The peasant carries a scythe in her right hand, and on her left arm an infant wrapped in a fringed shawl. Her kerchief is also a helmet, and her skirt also a shield. Her strong body stands firmly on the ground; her head and glance are proudly raised. The details are accurate and legible, but simplified into compact geometric masses. González employs a double emphasis: on narrative realism that renders this woman immediate and believable, and on heavy welded metal and abstract structure that turns her defiance into tangible weight. He thus creates in her the visible symbol of Republican resistance during the Spanish Civil War.

González refers to modern social history, Picasso to traditional iconography. His Man with Sheep is a modern Good Shepherd, religious only through allusion and indirection. The roughly modeled figure is powerful and self-contained, its weight resting on both legs. The sheep's twisted awkward mass projects from the man's upright body; in shape and surface their heads also contrast, one rigid and enclosed, the other in movement and amorphous. In the ancient Good Shepherd, the Lamb is at rest around Christ's shoulders. Here it struggles, yet appears subdued less by the man's physical strength than by his inner force. The inescapable reference to the past enriches the meaning of Picasso's modern group.

13

The Torso

The Walking Man by Rodin was modeled early in his career as a study for his *St. John the Baptist*. He did not originally think of it as a finished sculpture; it was a concentrated analysis of skeletal interlocking and muscular structure, necessary in his working out of the completed figure. It was cast in bronze and exhibited only many years later, in 1907, and even then was not readily accepted for itself. Today we see it as a whole work, and look upon it as we do later, twentieth-century torsos which were conceived as such.

Why does the modern artist deliberately create a fragment? The concept probably came from his admiration for once complete classical sculptures whose head and limbs had been broken off and lost, but which he (like some Renaissance artists) nevertheless found beautiful and expressive. Because parts of the body are missing, because, above all, the features of the face are absent, the artist must work entirely through humanity's common elements, and so render a necessarily anonymous body expressive in itself. There can be no escape into anecdote; therefore the form has to be altogether precise so that it can render a generalized meaning.

Maillol's *Ile de France* is a torso used as a symbol of the region around Paris, a modern city-state. Such a personification is in the classical mode, as is the emphasis upon restrained mass, smooth surface, and even flow of silhouette. There is a traditional "beauty" here, composing the sensuous appeal of the body, in contrast to Rodin's interest in articulated structure. Like the Rodin, Maillol's figure also conveys a sense of energy, but an energy animating the whole form rather than driving its interlocking parts, so that the figure floats as much as it strides.

14

opposite
Auguste Rodin
The Walking Man. 1877–78

right
Aristide Maillol
Ile de France (Torso). ca. 1910

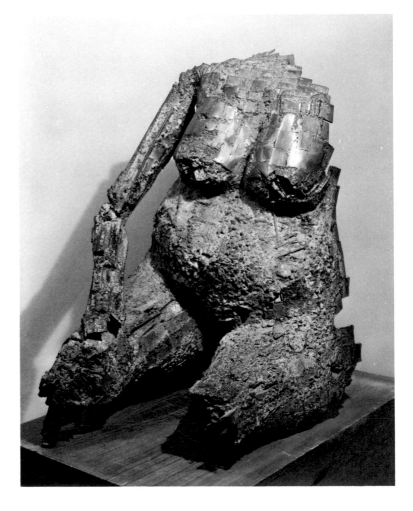

16

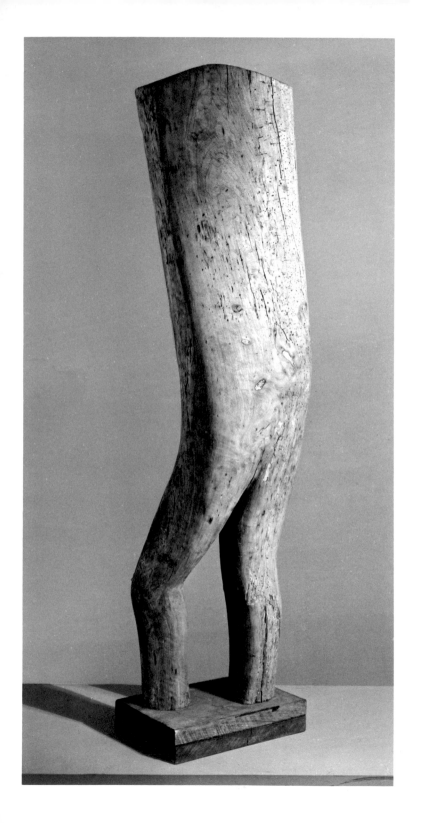

Lachaise arranged his *Torso* as a symmetrical silhouette. He has flattened the figure (seen from the back), narrowed the waist, enlarged the thrown-back shoulder blades and the buttocks, and created a molded relief at once organic and abstract. The fusion is reminiscent of certain prehistoric stone idols, symbols of fertility.

More recently sculptors have moved away from this concept of the clean, "completed" fragment, which, once created, exists whole and self-contained, toward its opposite—the ragged or unfinished fragment that continues to suggest, or to refer to, its missing parts. Hague's hesitant figure, its body cut somewhere between waist and neck, and legs that neither stand nor stride, seems a pathetic portion of a torso, denied even the dignity of a finished surface. César's seated torso is even more unlovely. Its aging forms are scarred and pitted; one arm is skeletal, the other missing, and the thighs end in jagged, open wounds. These "damaged" torsos recall us to the transience and anguish of the human condition.

opposite left
Gaston Lachaise
Torso. 1930

opposite right
César
Torso. 1954

left
Raoul Hague
Ohayo Wormy Butternut. 1947–48

17

The Reclining Figure

The four works illustrated here span thirty years of modern sculpture. They also represent four very different treatments of a theme that is almost as old as the standing figure. One associates the reclining nude with the classical styles of the past: the Ilyssos and the Fates of the Parthenon pediments, Roman river gods, or the garden statues of Versailles; but Bernini and other baroque sculptors dealt with it too. For the sculptor of the twentieth century these well-known older works constitute a familiar, but largely unconscious, background for his own interpretation, while certain key modern works provide a more immediate counterpoint.

The theme is the same, but the figures vary in their materials, their poses, and especially in how and how far they have been simplified and stylized. Yet each seems contained by a spatial box whose base is the plane on which the figure lies, and in each the masses of the body are composed in a balanced rhythm. We are thus made aware of a series of answering shapes, the "positive" ones of the parts of the body, and the "negative" ones of the intervening spaces.

Matisse recalls the curve of the hip in the outline of the shoulder, he repeats the bend of the knee in the angle of the elbow, and the volume of the breasts in the larger sphere of the head and hair. The left arm parallels the left thigh, the right arm, the hidden right thigh. Triangles bite into the silhouette at the waist, between head and shoulder, and find an echo in the space enclosed by the raised arm sharply bent back. But there is much more here than a silhouette. As the body twists upon itself, each part defines a slightly different diagonal, and the eye follows incipient movement into a realization of space.

opposite
Henri Matisse
Reclining Nude, I. 1907

right
Henry Moore
Reclining Woman. 1930

above
Julio González
Reclining Figure. 1934

opposite
Jacques Lipchitz
Reclining Nude with Guitar. 1928

Moore replaces animation with mass, subtlety with force. He insists upon the parallel sides of his original stone block, makes the figure so big and so right-angled that it almost touches them everywhere. He too uses repetitions: the cones of breasts and knees, the squareness of arms and shoulders, fists and feet. Simplified in its details, the figure has been enlarged to symbolic proportions. It is both inert and alive. Although stone is not yet entirely transmuted into flesh, some vital spirit seems to be awakening in the still heavy mass of this earth goddess.

Lipchitz summarizes his *Reclining Nude with Guitar* within a clear, continuous, decorative outline. Limbs, body, and head flow together; interior spaces match the shape of the outside contour. There is a rhythmic alternation of angles and curves, with a culminating contrast in the staccato relief of the guitar set against the body's legato forms.

Space invades González's *Reclining Figure* too, but while Lipchitz notes its intrusion in a witty shorthand, González allows it to reform the body into an architectural abstraction. Only hints remain of its source—the shape of the pelvis, the head with projecting strands of hair resting on the ground—and to recognize these one must have seen, in other works, how González developed his particular language of forms. But such recognition is not necessary to appreciate the strong rhythms and space-defining structure of this small but monumental figure.

The Head

The freedom of modern sculpture is well ex-
emplified in the five heads shown here. So is
its restraint and its severe and logical control
of form. Nature is in every case the starting
point, but it is not the observed image that
limits the sculptor's variations. Instead, those
limits are imposed by his imaginative purpose,
which provides direction, and by the internal
coherence of a formal structure which binds
the work's parts into a visible and evident
whole. In other words, a personal concept,
having only a tangential relation to our usual
way of seeing the world, draws the bounda-
ries of his creation.

Brancusi's *The New Born* symbolizes
human beginnings in formal simplicity, while
at the same time suggesting origins and
growth. With the mouth its only feature, the
smooth head portrays not one child, but all
infants. It is also an egg shape, with all that
this implies of birth. Its continuous form is
hardly interrupted by the single plane of the
face and the ridge of the forehead. It is at once
an organic and a geometric shape, and the high
polish of the marble gives to the solid, classic
weight we know the stone possesses an apparent shell-thin fragility.

For simplicity, Matisse's *Tiari* substitutes
humorous multiplication. He has started with
the same basic ovoid, joined nose and forehead in a bird-like form that in its own way
recalls the egg, and then repeated it with
variations in the billowing hairdo. The pro-
liferation of the decoration surmounting the
thrown-back head offers an ironic commentary on the proud face precisely by its formal
similarity. Here, so to speak, form criticizes
its own content.

opposite
Constantin Brancusi
The New Born. 1916

right
Henri Matisse
Tiari. 1930

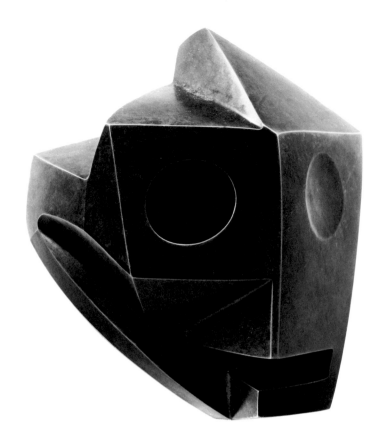

left
Julio González
Head. 1935?

above
Alberto Giacometti
Cubist Head. 1934–35

opposite
Pablo Picasso
Death's Head (Flayed Head). 1944

Brancusi and Matisse share a similar tangibility. González, as humorous as Matisse, draws only the contours: the back of the head, little strands of hair, the x-ray of a mouth with teeth, eyes projecting on two rods above a symbolic disk. This is a head penetrated by space and somehow reduced to its expression and its intelligence.

In Giacometti's *Cubist Head* these feelings of life and energy are displaced by a sense of the occult and the sinister, while Picasso's skull is a meditation upon death. Full forms give way to pierced and hollow surfaces. The left side of Giacometti's *Head,* though austere, is forceful; the right side, its flat planes cut away at forehead, nose and jaw, its eye-socket sunken (though not actually pierced, as in the Picasso), is fleshless. Thus the head combines life and death, as in some fifteenth-century German prints, or the representation of the Mexican god, Chacmool. Less geometric, more battered and lifeless, Picasso's *Death's Head* is no less a calculated modern morality, akin to those upon which the Spanish saints so often meditate. As in César's *Torso* (page 16), the apparent accidents, carefully controlled, express the frailty of the human organism.

The Portrait

Photography is often said to have removed the need for the portrait. Insofar as portraits in the past were simply more or less accurate documentary records, this is certainly true. But great portraits have always been much more than the skillful rendering of externals, and the penetration and interpretation of a complex character by a sensitive, perceptive observer is still valid and fascinating.

Such a portrait may be no less revealing for being highly subjective and may not require the model's actual presence. Rodin's *Baudelaire* was done after the death of the poet (whose work meant much to the sculptor), using a young artist as a model. "I cannot conceive of a statue of Baudelaire, . . . who lived only by his brain," said Rodin. "With him, the head is everything." The large forehead, bitter yet delicate mouth, and intense, visionary gaze directed as much inward as outward, are together a precise and subtle fusion of complex characteristics. Yet, as Rodin intended, it is the volume of the head that dominates.

Lachaise's *Marianne Moore* renders a very different sort of poetic spirit, young, assured, and seemingly without inward doubts and complications. The attractive features are given in detail; the slightly raised pose of the head, the direct glance, all suggest a certain eagerness, a direct desire to meet the outside world, and a confident optimism that the poet will be equal to the encounter.

Sintenis, in her *Self-Portrait,* presents herself in a much more somber light. The columnar-like neck, the frontal immobility of the gaze, the uneven line of the head, these suggest an ancient monument—Egyptian or early Greek; the changeable has been frozen into the unchanging. But this is also truly a portrait

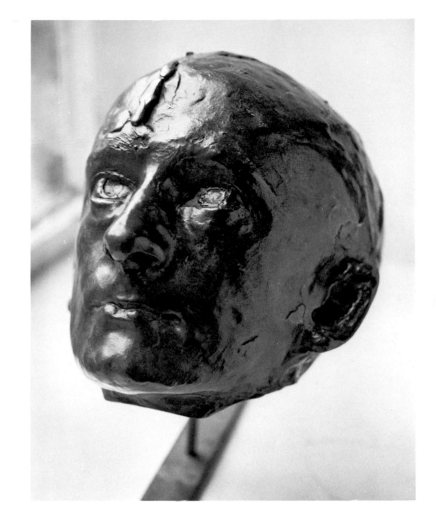

opposite
Auguste Rodin
Baudelaire. 1898

above left
Gaston Lachaise
Marianne Moore. 1924

above right
Renée Sintenis
Self-Portrait. 1945

left
Jacob Epstein
Oriel Ross. 1932

opposite
Marino Marini
Curt Valentin. 1953

done from life; with the pathos of an unwavering honesty, the artist has set down all the mortal effects of living.

Grace, and a certain ease and animation emanate from Epstein's portrait of *Oriel Ross*. He seems to have responded to his sitter's naturalness by recording it with equal naturalness—not an easy task. Using an overall rhythm of modeling and flow of light and shade, Epstein achieves character and unity through an altogether unstressed observation, evenly recorded.

Strain and intensity, so often present in the modern portrait, are seen again in Marini's *Curt Valentin*. And perhaps even self-doubt appears in this art dealer and defender of sculptors. The heavy head and neck have the force of an ancient Roman portrait. But the unequal eyes, the slightly open mouth, the whole indeterminate surface, convey a hesitant sensitivity in conflict with underlying strength.

Impressionism

Impressionist painters were interested in capturing the momentary. They rendered it through the informal poses of their figures and composition of their canvases, and especially through effects of color and light that tended to dissolve solid form. There thus can be no exact equivalent in sculpture.

Among the impressionist painters only Degas (and Renoir in his old age) did any sculpture. Degas's subjects were those of his paintings: horses, dancers, and women in the routine postures of their everyday lives. His *Dancer Putting on Her Stocking* has the hardly kept balance and the instability of the act itself, but none of its inherent tension. Degas transcribes no muscular pull or articulation. The freshness and vigor of his modeling deliberately remains on the surface, since he was more interested in the arabesque of outline and in the effects of light upon form than in the internal structure of that form. His flattened patches (originally in wax) render this diffusion of the atmosphere, and at the same time, independent of all representation, have a rhythmic life of their own.

Rosso's intentions were even more closely allied to those of the impressionist painters. In *The Bookmaker* the impreciseness of surface detail is an acknowledgment of an intervening atmosphere that diffuses the tangible form. The figure's slant suggests movement, the shifting, broad planes of light and dark, the impermanence of vision. Using his preferred medium of wax, Rosso has minimized the hard and tactile qualities of sculpture in favor of momentary appearance. To do this he has had to fix the position of the evanescent forms; *The Bookmaker* must be viewed from the front only, and lit only in a certain way, to reveal what is seen at a par-

opposite
Hilaire Germain Edgar Degas
Dancer Putting on Her Stocking. 1896–1911

right
Medardo Rosso
The Bookmaker. 1894

ticular moment in a particular environment.

Rodin captures the changing instant through the study of movement. Unlike Rosso, he is not concerned with atmospheric distortions; unlike Degas, he is interested in the tensions and compressions of bodily structure. He drew from the figure in motion, and his *Dance Movement D* records a difficult pose that will instantly change. In both composition and psychology the figure is concentrated upon itself. A single muscular effort draws the whole shape together, fusing head and body and obliterating any self-consciousness. The light reflections on the surface reveal internal tensions, and space exists only as making movement possible. The figure's visual balance (the stretched vertical against the cramped diagonals) grows out of its moment of physical poise, accurately rendered. Where, as in the hands, the awkward, even the ugly, will add vitality, Rodin employs it.

Auguste Rodin
Dance Movement D. 1911

Symbolism

Although based on the most careful observation, Rodin's immense *Monument to Balzac,* standing over nine feet high, unlike his dancer (page 32), goes well beyond naturalism toward an expressive symbolism. Rodin worked on this figure for some seven years. He recorded the features of Balzac's compatriots in his native Touraine, made successive studies of the head, of the nude body in various poses, and of the robe, before arriving at the final version. He sought to fuse identifying detail and meaningful posture into an eloquent visual symbol —of Balzac, and of all artistic creation. The features are those of Balzac, the loose, flowing robe is the voluminous dressing gown he wore when writing, and the proportions of the figure beneath it are his. But all the details of this accurate portrait—the size, the stance, the folds of cloth, the modeling of the head—are both enlarged and simplified. The impressive unbroken silhouette, carrying its energy into the lifted head, is at once defiant and receptive to the light of inspiration. "My principle," said Rodin, "is to imitate not only form but life and ... [to] amplify it by exaggerating the holes and lumps, to gain thereby more light, after which I search for a synthesis of the whole." Most of his contemporaries, expecting a conventional resemblance, could see only a shapeless mass, apparently unfinished, or else a caricature. But the head, although brutally simplified, can only be that of Balzac. And we have come to understand Rodin's intention: to celebrate, through Balzac, the vigor and the heroism of prolific genius.

We are more familiar with the parallels to such aims in the painting of the period. Gauguin, van Gogh, and even Seurat also wished to render states of feeling, and ideas, through the direct impact of artistic form. They

Auguste Rodin
Monument to Balzac. 1897

left
Émile-Antoine Bourdelle
Beethoven, Tragic Mask. 1901

opposite
Wilhelm Lehmbruck
Standing Youth. 1913

used external appearances as the equivalents of underlying emotion or ideal structure. Since the visual surface of their art stands for a non-visual reality, they have been called symbolists.

There is symbolism as well in Bourdelle's imaginary portrait *Beethoven, Tragic Mask*. He also portrays the defiant genius, but one who has paid for his difference from the crowd in loneliness and suffering, and whose twisted features express bitterness and despair. Bourdelle, Rodin's pupil and assistant, has learned well his teacher's lesson of sculpture as the art of the hollow and the lump; he has transformed the ridges and valleys of this face into a landscape of emotion, giving the lines of light and the pools and rivers of dark a rhythmic intensity of their own. The forms are powerful, but we are meant to look past them to the emotion they transcribe and symbolize.

Inner feeling also rules Lehmbruck's *Standing Youth*. The attenuated limbs, the bent head lifted free of the body, the deep-set eyes and high forehead are all outward signs of an inner spiritual life. While the stylizations of Rodin and Bourdelle express intense and positive emotion, Lehmbruck's thin, nervous line (related to art nouveau), the very meagerness of his forms, suggest contemplation and withdrawal. The calm and quiet pose of this somewhat decorative figure, its paradoxically harmonious gauntness, embody acceptance and resignation. Flesh and bone, instead of taking on the shape of energy, whether triumphant as with Rodin or anguished as with Bourdelle, are so subdued they seem almost to regret their own existence. Even Giacometti's light-consumed *Man Pointing* (page 11) belongs more positively to the material world.

Reactions to Rodin

During the first decade of the twentieth century, while Rodin was at the height of his fame, a number of younger sculptors developed new and opposing ideas. Although they reacted in different ways, they were generally agreed on one thing: whether the sculptor worked in bronze, or stone, or wood, "truth to materials" was his prime axiom. He had to respect the nature of his medium, be guided by its inherent qualities, and allow its character to be in constant evidence. In practice this meant closed rather than open form, stasis rather than movement, mass rather than animated surface, and as a result (in contrast to Rodin), a preference for carving over modeling.

Even where the actual technique of modeling was employed its effects were restrained to approximate carving. Thus both Bourdelle's monumental head and Maillol's nude figure, *The Mediterranean,* are in the tradition of the carved stone sculpture of classical antiquity. Bourdelle emphasizes the volume of the head, simplifies the features, divides the planes by unmistakable ridges. Neither tactilely nor optically is there any resemblance to flesh. If anything the plaster has been treated like stone. Maillol has so arranged the limbs of his figure that they are parallel to the strict limits of a confining cube, and within it a pyramidal arrangement carries the weight of the body to the ground in absolute repose. Except for a few highlights, the contained bronze forms might well be carved. A comparison with Matisse's *Reclining Nude* (page 18), with its freedom of pose and modeling, points up Maillol's calculated restraint.

For Bourdelle and Maillol the unity of the block is an abstract, regulating idea; for Brancusi it is a physical presence to be left undisturbed. He fits the two figures of *The Kiss*

38

above
Émile-Antoine Bourdelle
Eloquence. 1917

opposite
Aristide Maillol
The Mediterranean. 1902–5

left
Ernst Barlach
Man Drawing a Sword. 1911

opposite
Constantin Brancusi
The Kiss. 1908

within its cubic mass, carving away just enough to make them recognizable, leaving the pitted surface of the limestone squared off and unpolished. Maillol's classic simplicity here gives way to more elemental forms. Inspired by the roughed-out figures of the early Middle Ages, whose low relief maintains the original outer envelope of the quarried block, Brancusi has used similarly stylized shapes to express age-old emotion. The extreme geometric simplification is the visual embodiment of mankind's enduring primitive core. Thus Brancusi's intuition paralleled the teachings of a developing psychology and anthropology, while he arrived at a language of form fundamental to later sculpture.

Barlach's *Man Drawing a Sword* makes use of another early tradition—the medieval wood sculpture of his native Germany. The direct and "honest" methods of the craftsman are made apparent by the marks of the chisel and the grain of the wood, and their pattern also serves a unifying function. The heavy symmetrical composition and bluntness of forms parallel the uncomplicated emotions of the subject. The archaizing theme and costume, the forceful peasant figure, also imply the ancient and the elemental. Less mysterious than the Brancusi, this is a more programmatic sculpture, hinting at both religion and revolt.

Cubism

Cubist sculpture in its beginnings was closely dependent on cubist painting. Picasso's *Woman's Head* is approximately his painted *Head* of about the same time. Rounded volumes and continuous surfaces have been flattened into a series of abrupt planes. Alternately advancing and receding, they first catch, then hide, the light, and the ridges where they meet define the head in clearly drawn lines. Slight depressions (of the cheek and neck, for example) are deepened until one can only guess at their shapes. This is Rodin's art "of the hollow and the lump," with the lumps sharpened between the increased hollows. The usual continuity of modulated volumes is thus replaced by a sequence of compartmentalized areas defined by contours at the edges where they meet. Light and shade are used less to convey the presence of solid volume and reflecting surface than to indicate an analytic structure drawn in space. At the same time, the resulting rhythmic sequence imposes on the head its own abstract logic of repeated curves brought to a sudden halt. Picasso's geometric treatment can be contrasted with both Rodin's more impressionist *Baudelaire* (page 26) and Matisse's more sensuous *Tiari* (page 23). Its mixture of hard and soft, of curve and straight line, is characteristic for cubism.

Certain areas in *Woman's Head* have turned into their opposites: the planes between the right jawbone and cheekbone, and just above the left side of the chin, have been indented, though in fact they protrude. Such substitution of the concave for the convex has been given more fluid and decorative handling in Archipenko's *Woman Combing Her Hair,* where it is especially evident in the legs and thighs. The slight shade that would indeed be cast by the rounded form has been rendered by

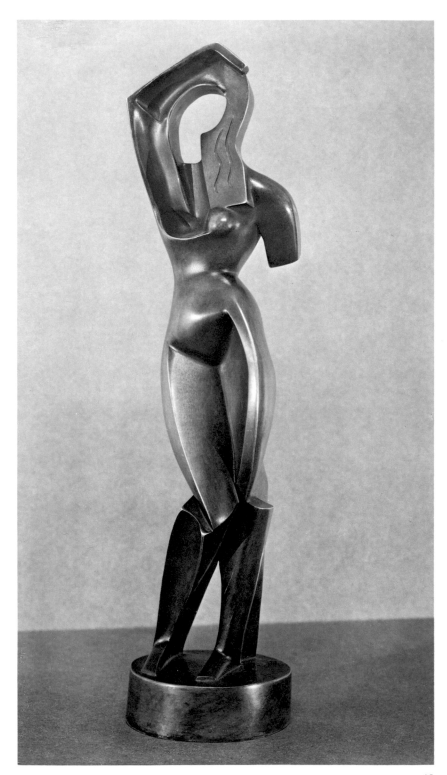

opposite
Pablo Picasso
Woman's Head. 1909

right
Alexander Archipenko
Woman Combing Her Hair. 1915

43

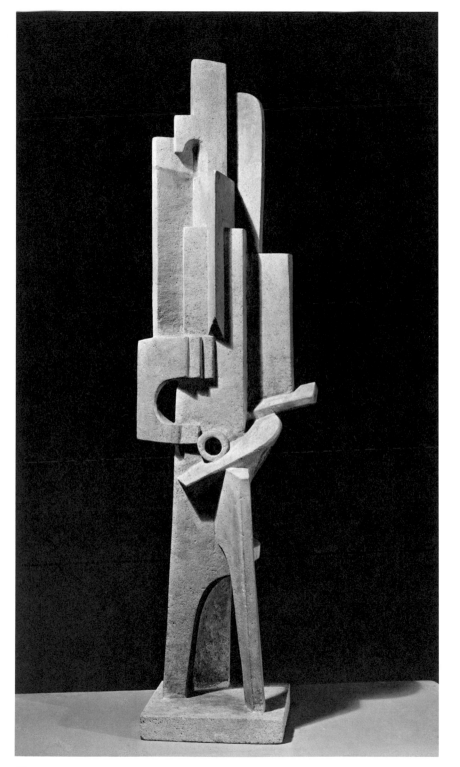

left
Jacques Lipchitz
Man with a Guitar. 1915

opposite
Henri Laurens
Head. 1918

a scooping out of the whole volume. We are intended to recast this "deformation" of nature back into its opposite. And we are meant to do the same where a void has been substituted for a solid, as in the head, or where our vision completes the absent curve of the left arm down to the thigh. Thus penetrated by light, the masses seem to shift in space.

Most cubist sculpture remains within the limits of such semi-naturalistic stylizations, and is generally also dominated by curved and flattened silhouettes. Only occasionally is it carried further, as in Lipchitz's *Man with a Guitar* where the general proportions of the human figure—head, torso and projecting elbow, legs—are still preserved, and the separated parts of the guitar are recognizable. But all these elements have been recomposed into an architectonic structure of interpenetrating planes. They have become almost entirely abstract schematized signs, whose reminiscent meaning for the artist is best understood by following their increasing stylization in a series of works. The flat surfaces, intersecting at right angles, imply their hidden continuations and so compel us to examine their relations from all sides. It is, finally, through the character of this interlocking geometric structure, independent of all representational associations, that the work commands our attention.

Laurens's *Head,* constructed from assembled parts, uses cubist principles to transform sculpture in the round into high relief. Receding planes—the nose, the left cheek, the rectangles of the head—are rotated toward the viewer to reduce foreshortening. The right eye and its framing trapezoid, and the right ear have been brought all the way forward to give a full view of both sides of the face. Depth is, however, added to this flattened design as if it were indeed a painting by applying color to produce the illusion of recession and projection, while its elements remain spread out to

left
Rudolf Belling
Sculpture. 1923

opposite
Ossip Zadkine
Mother and Child. 1918

46

be measured by the eye. The result is a play between art and reality: the constructed *Head* is flatter than any real-life cranium but appears to be deeper than it actually is. The larger, starker forms first eliminate all nuance, and are then relieved by a burst of irregular design. Both kinds of witty paradox are very much in the cubist spirit.

Although advanced in style, cubism was traditional in subject matter. The harlequins, the guitar players, the figures, the still lifes that were its usual themes were familiar in the studio but had little connection with the modern elements in the ordinary man's environment. Belling's *Sculpture* tries to bridge this gap. It employs the cubist vocabulary of geometric shapes and interpenetrating planes, and even approaches cubist painting in a transparency that permits a simultaneous view of overlapping areas. But its materials are industrial, and its geometric elements have the shape and weight, the precise cut and high finish of machine-made parts. There is acknowledgment of the visual and emotional impact of modern industry and its new techniques. Léger's paintings of the same period offer a parallel.

Zadkine's *Mother and Child* also stylizes its subject to the frontier of abstraction. Its characteristic use of depression and protuberance emphasizes contrasts rather than sequences, as in Picasso's *Woman's Head*. The left arm and right breast employ a typical reversal (concave to be read as convex) arising from an analysis of interpenetrating structure and space. The suckling infant's head is also the mother's breast. Here, as elsewhere, the cubist artist avoids the leanness of descriptive enumeration; through ambivalent form and evocative suggestion he wishes to preserve the multiplicity of both structure and meaning.

Futurism

Futurism wished at all costs to shake itself loose from the past, and it thought of the present largely in terms of energy, motion, and intensity. Its general program (first pronounced by the Italian writer Marinetti) glorified the "dangerous life" (including violence and war), enthusiastically accepted modern civilization, and stressed the beauty of machinery. Manifestoes preceded works of art. For the futurist artist the portrayal of movement, force, and the passage of time were as much means of rendering personal emotion as of analyzing the visual world. From the cubists the futurists learned how to take the forms of an object apart and then recompose its different aspects into a single, simultaneous representation, but they extended the method to suggest motion, and through motion intense feeling. They rendered dynamic direction by allusive "lines of force," and, extending the principle of simultaneity, suggested the fusion of an object with its surroundings by a further compenetration of planes.

It was difficult to put such abstract notions into visual terms, and even harder to put them into the concrete medium of sculpture. Not surprisingly, the Manifesto of Futurist Sculpture (1912), followed the painting manifesto by two years. Written by Boccioni, it included these lines: "Sculpture must give life to objects by making their extension in space palpable, systematic, and plastic, since no one can any longer believe that an object ends where another begins. . . . We therefore cast all aside and proclaim the absolute and complete abolition of definite lines and closed sculpture. We break open the figure and enclose it in environment."

Boccioni's ideas are vividly embodied in his *Unique Forms of Continuity in Space*. His

Umberto Boccioni
Unique Forms of Continuity in Space
1913

left
Raymond Duchamp-Villon
The Horse. 1914

opposite
Alexander Archipenko
Struggle (Boxing). 1914

purpose has been to modernize a conventional theme and give it life "by making visible its prolongation into space." He has tried to show not the "construction of the body" (that would be static), but the "construction of the actions of the body," by using "a kind of spiral, centrifugal architecture which would serve as a plastic equivalent for the dynamics of organic action," and by visualizing the "lines of force" in the swirling shapes pressed back by the figure's forward rush.

Duchamp-Villon's *Horse* is a synthesis of cubism and futurism, less static than the one, more abstract than the other. He has recast the horse, an age-old symbol of movement and passion, in modern terms by joining mechanical and organic forms, thus suggesting a more powerful, more contemporary dynamism. Instead of Boccioni's stylized equivalents of movement, Duchamp-Villon makes use of more concentrated abstract forms, further from their sources in nature and freely combined. His purpose is not to give the illusion of movement (the composition remains static) but rather to suggest latent dynamic force.

Futurist inspiration also transforms the cubist elements of Archipenko's *Struggle (Boxing)*. From cubism come the combination of flat and rounded surfaces, and the introduction of space at the center. But the virile subject, and the strong directional lines and interpenetrating forms that suggest the action and the fusion of opposing forces, are altogether futurist in spirit.

Dada and Surrealism

The impressionists thought of art as "nature seen through a temperament," that is, the world carefully observed and interpreted through the eyes of a particular individual. Cubism went farther: its "deformations" and rearrangements, although never completely abstract, clearly imply that interpretation is freed from immediate observation and that the artist creates a new kind of reality, which is given its coherence and meaning by human association, memory, and imagination. Dada and surrealism adopt and expand this world of art in which the play of the mind is paramount. What counts is the creative imagination; the artist is someone who can impose that imaginative vision, and he is free to do so in any way that succeeds. He is freed from copying nature, and he is also freed from the limitations of traditional technique; his skill as a craftsman is measured entirely by the imaginative results he achieves.

Dada's expression of these assumptions is here illustrated by two works which, although they fall outside the dates of the group movement (roughly 1915–22), well embody its attitudes. Duchamp exercised no physical skills in the fabrication of his "readymade," *Bottle Rack*. As its name makes clear it is an industrial object, one of many made to serve an altogether practical function. Duchamp's "artistry" has entered, not into its making, but into its recognition and selection. He has isolated it from its familiar practical context and posed it, forcing us to contemplate it. By treating it like a work of art, he has transformed it into one, or at least a simulacrum of one. Not every object is susceptible to such a metamorphosis, only those with certain "mysterious" (that is, largely unconscious) qualities of form and association. He whose awareness of himself

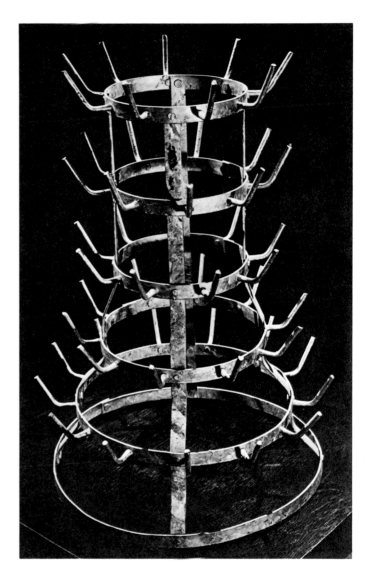

opposite
Marcel Duchamp
Bottle Rack. 1914

above
Pablo Picasso
Bull's Head. 1943

above left
Alberto Giacometti
The Couple. 1926

above right
David Hare
Man with Drums. 1947

opposite
Max Ernst
Lunar Asparagus. 1935

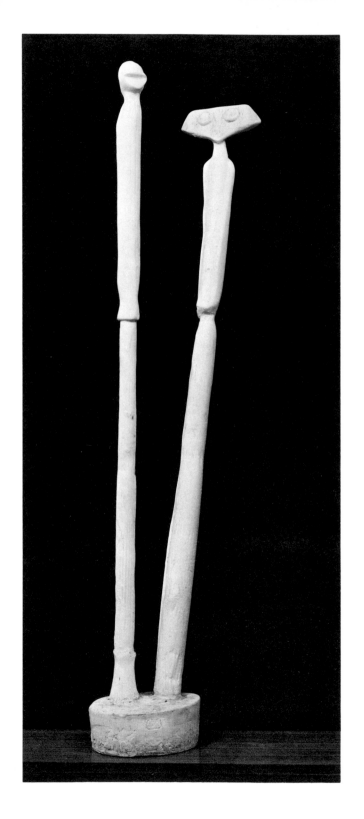

and the world enables him to make the proper choices is an artist.

Similarly, the fabrication of Picasso's *Bull's Head* involved no physical labor and one single act—of the imagination. Picasso had the wit to see how he could put together the saddle and handlebars of an old bicycle into an evocative new object. Part of the fascination of the new creation lies precisely in its old parts being unaltered, while their combination changes them altogether. They oscillate between their past and present existences.

Technically, Giacometti's *The Couple* and Ernst's *Lunar Asparagus* are traditional sculptures. But their distance from nature is considerable. Giacometti uses a number of simplifications, barely recognizable signs that distinguish the sexes of the two figures and also distinguish a more solid character from one more supple. Ernst's pair is equally but more subtly differentiated. Both artists have employed the surrealist method of implying more than is presented and bringing the imagination into play. Giacometti has referred to the symbolic ritual figures of ancient cultures, somehow infusing the impersonal with the self-conscious and endowing them with dignity and humor. Ernst's title so aptly joins the strange shapes to a strange meaning that the two isolated yet related presences call forth mysterious nocturnal worship; yet, like Giacometti's figures, they do not take themselves entirely seriously.

Hare's *Man with Drums* makes more specific use of the surrealist "double image." It joins subject, memory, and meaning into a single vision. The drummer's occupation has so possessed him that he has become one with his instrument. He is as a child or a poet might remember him, a drummer-man. In this way the artist projects the shifts and fusions that take place within what he has called "the spaces of the mind."

Biomorphism

The works shown on these pages were created over a span of three decades and belong to no single "school." Clearly, each has its own character, but the many traits they have in common indicate that they are part of a continuing tendency.

The curve, whether of line or of surface, is basic to them all; it constitutes the sole, or the dominant, formal language employed. Besides, these forms, whether they define more or less stylized representations, or are altogether nonrepresentational, are seemingly more organic than geometric. Either they are obviously derived from the shapes of living forms, or, being abstract, they still have the tightness, the tension, the apparent pull from within, limiting extension, that brings to mind organic structure.

In all these works, too, there is a strong sense, not only of surrounding, but of invading space. Where material mass is cut away, is indented or hollowed out, it leaves a space that the eye follows and encloses, that is, so to speak, made present by its absence. We have already met this interaction of mass and space, of positive and negative volume. It is one of the controlling qualities of cubism, and its consciousness continues here.

In *Adam and Eve* Brancusi's interest in growth and fertility is again evident (as it was in *The New Born*, page 22), expressed through a few simple forms. His hewn wooden shapes are only distantly representational, recalling portions of the human figure in a generalized and symbolic way. Brancusi was among the first to admire African sculpture, though he imitated none of its details. Here the variations on the sphere, arranged on a vertical axis, are related to certain African compositional rhythms, as well as to those of cubism. Both

56

opposite
Constantin Brancusi
Adam and Eve. 1921

right
Jacques Lipchitz
Song of the Vowels. 1931–32

Henri Laurens
Crouching Figure. 1940

modes have been reduced to their essentials. "Simplicity is not a goal in art," he wrote, "but, in spite of oneself, one arrives at simplicity as one gets close to the real meaning of things."

Lipchitz's more figurative *Song of the Vowels* also attains a symbolic reduction of representational elements. By balancing the solid weight of the leaning figure against the open curves of the instrument, he has infused static mass with incipient movement. Heavy as this large group is, space has invaded it, and it seems about to float through space. First seen as separate, player and harp fuse into a single contrapuntal composition, from which successive waves emanate toward its limits, and even then appear to continue invisibly beyond. Lipchitz has used the cubist understanding of the interpenetration of planes, of the alternation of solid and void, to organize the remarkable animation of this enormous semi-abstract form.

By contrast, Laurens's *Crouching Figure* is all heavy, lethargic, turned in upon itself, belonging to the earth rather than the sky. Though its parts swell and bulge, they are bound by a narcissistic concentration; though they are all organic forms, they are hardly differentiated so that there is no controlling center, and head and thighs, breasts and elbows, resemble one another; the figure seems to have grown by the multiplication of one bulbous shape, its form constrained by the stretching of its skin. It is a figure that must be seen from all sides, since its forms twist and reverse themselves. In its various parts there is no straight line, yet for all its curves the total mass is contained within a limiting cube and struggles against the pressure of its defining volume. The dual principle of cubism thus again plays a determining role.

Every element of Arp's *Human Concretion*, like each part of *Crouching Figure*, is made to lead a double existence: its own life as

59

above
Jean Arp
Human Concretion. 1935

below
Henry Moore
Two Forms. 1934

opposite
Barbara Hepworth
Head (Elegy). 1952

60

a unique form, newly created by the artist, and a secondary life dependent upon its reminding us of a form already existing in nature. Some meeting of the two extremes is present in all art; it is characteristic of cubism that it balances one off against the other, and takes pleasure in a shifting awareness of the two together. Arp's reference to human forms is less specific than Laurens's, but it cannot be called more abstract; his creative invention moves, not away from, but toward nature. Arp said, "We wish to produce as a plant produces its fruit, and not to re-produce.... Since there is not the slightest trace of abstraction in our art, we call it *art concret*."

There is no need for the sculptor to go even this far in the direction of representation, as Moore's *Two Forms* demonstrates. Without recalling any single plant or animal, these curved shapes are closer to the configurations of living forms than to those of inert matter. It is not too much to say that across an intervening distance the two forms pay attention to each other. That interval had its origins in the holes first pierced by Archipenko (page 43) and Lipchitz (page 44); here it has expanded to flow freely around the detached element. But although physically separate the two forms are visually—and psychologically—joined. Mass and void (positive and negative volumes) have become answering entities; they have pulled just this far apart and can pull no farther.

In the *Head (Elegy)* by Hepworth, space is spanned and measured by the more analytic device of the stretched strings. By defining oblique planes in depth while still allowing the light to come through, they tell us that the shape of space, while intangible, is as important as that of the material that surrounds it. This is a device related to constructivist techniques, employed as a geometric contrast to the enclosing biomorphic forms.

Ease and apparent improvisation mark the bent planes of Calder's *Whale*. Carefully, almost symmetrically composed, they twist and turn with a casual air, as if this just happened to be one pose among many; enormously heavy, they rise from the ground as if weightless. The name too seems like a sudden discovery, exactly right and yet unnecessary. (This might as well be a jungle plant.) From these contradictions comes a contradictory creation—at once mechanical and organic, serious and witty.

Alexander Calder
Whale. 1937

Constructivism

Traditionally, sculptors have thought in terms of mass and volume. The conventional techniques of carving and modeling result in forms which occupy a certain volume and have or suggest a certain weight. We talk of form and space as opposites, or as positive and negative. Space is only implied, since the sculpture's presence is measured by its displacement. That some works seem "lighter" or "airier" than others (they may in fact be the opposite), indicates that mass is still the standard of reference and space remains peripheral.

Constructivism repudiates these traditional conceptions. We have already seen space penetrating a sculpture's mass, not simply interrupting it, but interacting with it (Lipchitz, page 57), and sculptural forms reaching out to include surrounding space (Boccioni, page 49). The constructivists (partly inspired by the ideas of futurism) make space the essential basis of their art; they wish to replace opaque mass by perceptible space, to make the void visible. They consider sculpture produced by conventional methods, no matter how stylized, to be naturalistic, static, and subjective, because it reflects personal feeling. Their own work is "realistic," because it is based on the realities of space and time; "dynamic," because by "the flow of lines and shapes" it includes kinetic rhythms; and "objective," because it reflects the true nature of the universe. In their Realistic Manifesto of 1920, Gabo and Pevsner renounced "volume . . . and mass as sculptural elements," and asserted that "depth [is] the one form of space." Their art is influenced by modern physics and geometry, but it is not a visualization of science. They are poets of space: "We do not measure works with the yardstick of beauty, we do not weigh them with pounds of tender-

64

Kasimir Meduniezky
Construction Number 557. 1919

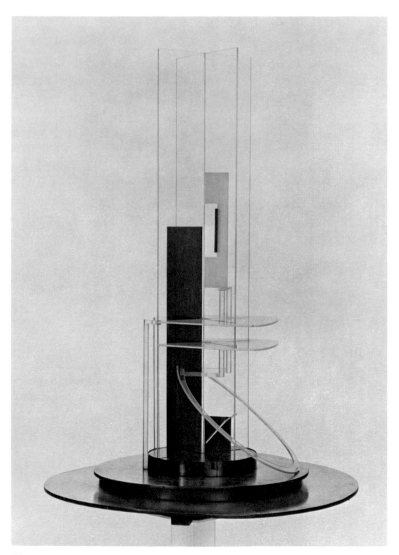

left
Naum Gabo
Column. 1923

opposite
Naum Gabo
Spiral Theme. 1941

ness and sentiment. . . . The realization of our perception of the world in the forms of space and time is the only aim of our . . . art."

Constructivism started in Russia, and its program reflected the early post-Revolutionary idealism. It believed the new utopian society demanded a new art, based on contemporary scientific thought and employing only modern materials. (But in 1922 the government suppressed the movement, saying it was of no service to the state.) Meduniezky's *Construction* belongs to this early stage, and its simple use of basic elements stands for a whole program. The familiar circle and triangle are reasonable forms, but placed in unstable equilibrium; they contrast with the larger, intuitively conceived curves. The medium has been reduced to a minimum; the iron bands simply outline an interplay of air volumes. The only filled form, the triangle, resting obliquely on its point, seems to cut through rather than to limit space. The massive cube, solid and opaque, enhances the sense of lightness and of play, at once free and calculated.

Gabo's *Column* was made just after he left Russia for Germany. Constructed of glass, metal, wood, and plastic, it is in the spirit of architecture (its concepts in fact influenced later architecture) but is conceived as pure art. Gabo had protested: "Either build functional houses and bridges or create pure art or both. Don't confuse one with the other." The interlocking transparent planes bring into focus a series of interpenetrating spatial volumes, defining, but hardly interrupting them. Only the simplest forms are used; there is a sure sense of interval and opposition, both in the proportions and in the stages leading from the opaque through translucence to light. Utterly serious in its intention, and constructed of symbolically modern materials, *Column* has been executed with a delicate touch; the result is a grave and lyrical work.

The elements of *Column* are the circle and the rectangle; there is a clear contrast between horizontal and vertical, mediated only by the obliquely placed ring. *Spiral Theme* is handled with the same restraint, but it is fluid rather than static. Because its basic geometry is more difficult to grasp, it seems less calculated, although its geometric reasoning is in fact just as careful. Since it is constructed of plastic, its planes never altogether block each other out but vary in translucence as our angle of vision changes. Seeing through each, we see them all; and as we trace their courses, at once behind and in front of each other, there is change and apparent movement. This is the "flow of lines and shapes" that prompted Gabo to state: "Constructive sculpture is not only three-dimensional, it is four-dimensional in so far as we . . . bring the element of time into it."

These same qualities are also present in Moholy-Nagy's *Space Modulator*, made of plexiglass and wire. But now the emphasis is on the spontaneous and the unexpected. The hand-modeled surfaces follow the artist's sudden impulse, the wires spread and extend like arbitrary veins, and sobering rules have been cast aside. Nevertheless the work embodies the ideas of constructivism. Moholy-Nagy said of it: "This composition demonstrates three types of transparent walls, circumscribed by the thick edges of the plastic or wire. One is moderately transparent (rhodoid), the second perfectly transparent (plexiglass), and the third supertransparent (air)."

Developable Column by Pevsner is based on the same "realist" principles as the two constructions by his brother Gabo. It gets its name because it is a variation on "developable surfaces," surfaces like those of the cone or the cylinder produced by the simple curving of a flat plane which could be extended indefinitely—characteristics suggested by the lines from whose development the surfaces are

László Moholy-Nagy
Space Modulator. 1940

69

above
Antoine Pevsner
Developable Column. 1942

opposite
Robert Jacobsen
Hengist. 1953

70

made. Despite certain geometrical affinities, such works are not to be confused with machines or even terrestrial mechanics: "Spatial construction and its aims," Pevsner wrote, "are not measured by the divisions of a yardstick: the eye is the principle means of measurement by which common sense can contemplate the infinities of space. Space is a poetry which is felt rather than measured. It reveals itself suddenly and entirely."

Constructivist attitudes need not always be so pure and so logical. Jacobsen's *Hengist,* as its heroic Saxon name implies, although materially and spatially altogether a construction, embodies a poetry of a different kind. It starts with deliberation and clarity in its rectangles, into whose framework are fitted more subjective forms, arranged in an almost impulsive way. The contained freedom of Meduniezky's early *Construction* is here echoed in a more massive fashion.

Space Drawing

The constructivists were the first to make the realization of space central to both their theory and their work, but it has been the basic concern of many modern sculptors. These other artists, while equally engaged in making space visible through their constructions, and themselves influenced by the constructivists, have been less programmatic in their ideas, and more directly intuitive in their solutions. Thus their varied works belong to no single school; but they do group themselves into several very general tendencies. One of these may be called space drawing. Whereas Gabo and Pevsner, in different ways, render space discernible through shaping it by planes, these artists instead employ connected lines and points to give discernible structure to the volumes they are limiting. It is as if the pencil or the pen, drawn through the air in three dimensions, had left behind a permanent record of its path. By following this visible trace, the eye grasps the forms it defines; in this way space is very nearly made tangible.

Picasso's *Construction in Wire* is such a space drawing, with roots in his earlier collage constructions. It is first of all an abstract arrangement of rods, seen initially as two-dimensional triangles, rectangles, and a circle. Joined, these grow together into three-dimensional forms and constitute a series of transparent, overlapping, intersecting cages; within their intriguing intricacy we try to make out some simple logic. In this task we fail, and are, of course, supposed to fail, since the transparency makes possible simultaneous, contradictory connections, edges of space that answer and complete a series of other edges, and so compose a number of different configurations, all equally valid. Finally, out of the many lines of construction emerges the suggestion of a

Pablo Picasso
Construction in Wire. 1928–29

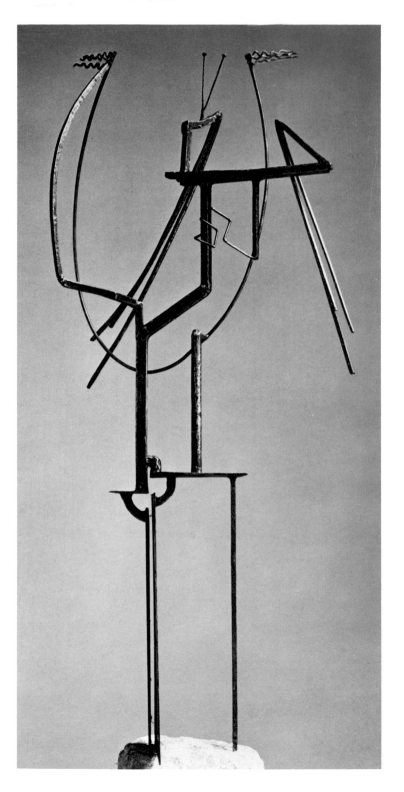

left
Julio González
Woman Combing Her Hair. 1930–33

opposite
Alberto Giacometti
The Palace at 4 A.M. 1932–33

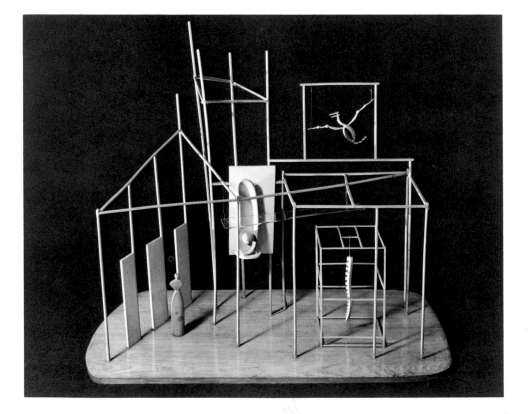

human figure which is perhaps the distant recollection of an ancient charioteer. By this witty metamorphosis of abstraction into representation, the spirit of dada is made to inhabit an otherwise spare composition.

In *Woman Combing Her Hair* (1930–33), González proceeds in the opposite direction: he starts with figuration and reduces it by abstraction to the bare elements of linear outline. The face becomes an oval, open at the top; the eyes, themselves become projected lines of sight, move out from an internal nerve center, and become a symbol of activity like that used in his *Head* (page 24). The hair streams in all directions—in small waves at the temples, in long strands toward the back, and symmetrically at the side. The result is a shorthand, at once humorous, legible, and abstract. "The important problem," González wrote, "is not only to make a work which is harmonious and perfectly balanced. No! But to get this result by the marriage of *material and space,* by the union of real forms with imaginary forms, obtained or suggested by established points . . . and, according to the natural law of love, to mingle them and make them inseparable . . . as are the body and the spirit."

A similar union joins the strange and disparate parts of *The Palace at 4 A.M.* It is a building drawn in outline only, a skeletal architecture through which space flows freely, inhabited by a few disquieting creatures, who though measurably isolated are psychologically connected. It is also a construction filled with air and mystery, occupied, yet disturbingly empty. An intuitive and visionary logic brings all these parts together. As Giacometti has said, here is a "freely associated dream fantasy," in which the "dominant factor is the basic form in its strange space relationships." Grasped visually, these relationships become symbolic; they have a meaning that can hardly be analyzed because, having been uncon-

sciously conceived, it "lives in its surreality."
"Once the object is constructed, I tend to see
in it, transformed and displaced, facts which
have profoundly moved me, often without my
realizing it." For us the meaning is conveyed
by scale, position, and interval, which combine
to create a double sense of trapped isolation
and involvement across a void. The effective
realization of the originally unprompted vision
demands exactness, and a "precise mechanism
which is of no use" (such as this one) must be
meticulously made.

Compared to the weight and solidity of
traditional sculptural methods, space drawing
is inherently light and open. Calder's mobile
carries this effect to the point of buoyancy.
Very large, made of steel and aluminum suspended from a single point, it seems to stay in
the air of its own accord. The fish-tail forms,
hung at the ends of a series of wires, balance
the heavier weight of the schematic lobster
trap, so that with the slightest movement of
the air the whole construction gently turns and
rocks. In this way its moving parts trace a constantly changing configuration, since their relations—to each other and to the external eye
—are unceasingly altered. Calder's mobile
swims in the air as the creatures of its title
would swim in the sea. Its patterns result from
a curious collaboration: the exact mechanics
of the artist who has poised these forms, and
the changing breezes that swing them around.
Like the dada sculptor, Calder accepts the limits of his artistic control, and then makes a
happily calculated use of chance.

Lippold's *Variation Number 7: Full Moon*
is, in contrast, a tightly planned and reasoned
work. Although it is physically lighter than
Calder's mobile, since its wires and rods reduce the material to a minimum and are indeed meant to suggest the immaterial, it is not
light-hearted. The design of these stretched
lines depends upon their continuing tension,

Alexander Calder
Lobster Trap and Fish Tail. 1939

left
Richard Lippold
Variation Number 7: Full Moon.
1949–50

opposite
Ibram Lassaw
Kwannon. 1952

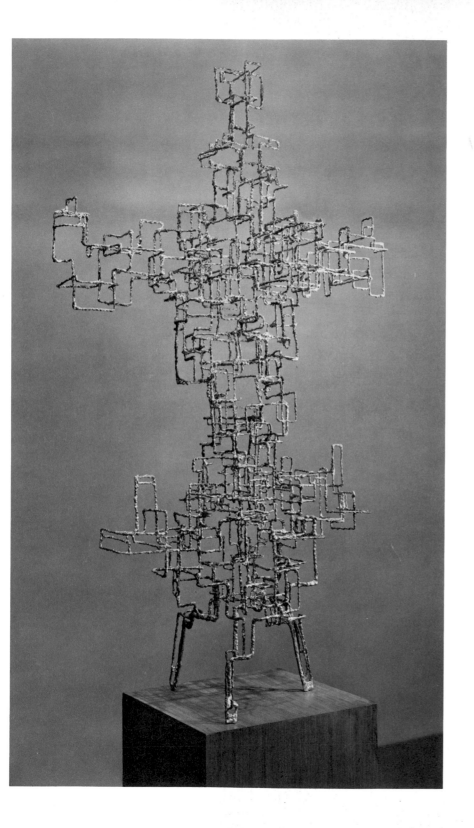

rather than on the resistance (compression) of most sculpture. Visually and physically they all depend upon one another, and within this "three-dimensional knitting" no single detail can be left to inspiration or all will become unraveled. From this contradiction between matter's reduction and a dependence on its strength (which is literally stretched to its utmost) comes a kind of determined and shivering rigidity. Lippold said that the "materials" of the twentieth century are space, time, and energy, and his woven, symmetrical constructions are intended as metaphors and models of our understanding of the universe.

If *Full Moon*, for all its gossamer quality, reflects a planned determination, *Kwannon,* more varied in the thicknesses and color of its metallic drawing, is also more relaxed in its design. Where Lippold dictates to his material, Lassaw allows it some part in his invention. The geometric structure of this work, even its stability, seem to have been reached in a meandering way, as though each small rectangle, open or closed, had simply suggested the next. The final overall design appears less the execution of a plan known in advance than a discovery that took shape as the work proceeded. There is here only an approximate geometry of uneven drawing, changing light reflection, and never repeated, never quite matching, but still similar, linked parts. Altogether abstract, *Kwannon* possesses as much an organic as an analytic unity.

Technically, most space drawings are constructions; that is, they are made of separate elements which are attached at clearly discernible joints and intersections. Most employ straight lines, but this is true even of those in which the curve predominates, as in Calder's mobile. De Rivera's *Construction 8,* on the contrary, is all of one piece. Its three-dimensional curve proceeds through space in a long, smooth, continuous flow, both its vitality

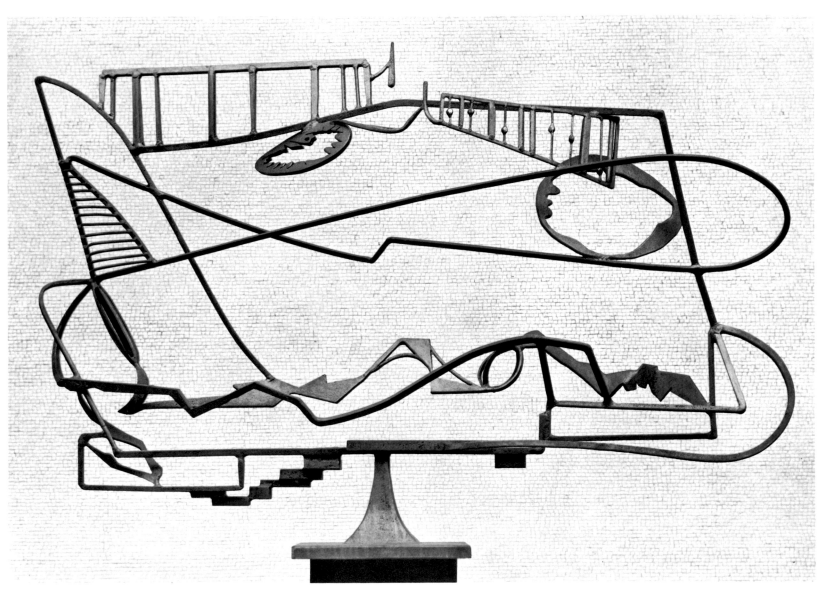

and elegance enhanced by its gradually varying diameter. As it turns on its single-pointed base, highlights and shadows move and change on its polished surface and play an active role in the definition of its form.

Space drawing is usually organized around a center. Though it is by its nature transparent, and generally not entirely symmetrical, it directs our attention from a traced periphery inward, and then out again; its depth is self-contained. In contrast, *Hudson River Landscape* fixes a single plane. Its origin in a synthesis of "drawings made on ten trips . . . on a train between Albany and Poughkeepsie" is evident in its varying lines—thick and thin, drawn out or blotted—forming a contour that encloses a self-contained composition. But the title refers to more than the occasion of the work. In arresting the eye it also dramatizes a distant perspective and gives romantic emphasis to a receding landscape space.

opposite
David Smith
Hudson River Landscape. 1951

below
José de Rivera
Construction 8. 1954

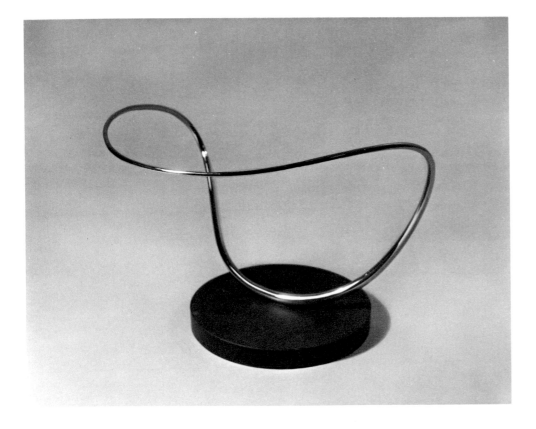

Expressionist Constructivism

The constructivist approach to sculpture is also basic to another tendency—less analytic and more emotional than space drawing—which similarly rejects the traditional carved or modeled mass and form. The term expressionist constructivism will serve to suggest a general direction loosely linking many artists of varying individual character and techniques. Although these sculptors share a concern for visually shaped space, first explored by the constructivists, they are less restricted in their methods and more subjective in their purposes. Where the constructivists wish to say (or to reveal) something about the nature and structure of the universe, these artists are more concerned with the symbolic expression of human emotion. Therefore, without ever making use of obvious representation, they again introduce references to natural and to geometric forms—and to the human figure. Thus they employ the interaction of space and surface (and occasionally, mass) to create fluid, open, asymmetrical compositions that, even when abstract, have the value of gesture and, through movement, convey feeling.

González's *Woman Combing Her Hair* (1936) is an early and influential example. Compared to his previous treatment of the same subject (page 74), which is constructed in outline only, this work has portions of considerable bulk. The lower section, contrasting with the flaring streamers of head and hair, suggests the mass of the body. Moreover, the volumes that indicate the stance, the twist of the torso, and then the large curve that is at once raised arm and facial outline, are freer in themselves and more freely arranged than formerly. The humor of the earlier version grows out of objective analysis, and so is geometric and fragmented; here there is a continuity and

Julio González
Woman Combing Her Hair. 1936

left
David Smith
Tank Totem V. 1955–56

opposite
Seymour Lipton
Sea King. 1956

substance that permits us an ironic identification with the figure. And this in turn gives the whole work its expressionist inflection.

Tank Totem V by David Smith, made of separate, welded iron parts, and therefore quite literally "constructed," is still further removed from the human figure. Nevertheless the reference to it by this rhythmic combination of disks and rectangles penetrated by space is both unmistakable and essential. The human suggestion, arising from legs and round body, and from the gesturing appendages (part arms, part lance), remains present even as it is absorbed into the abstract, openwork structure. The geometric forms, although they are related to the mathematics of constructivism, point directly to the menacing machinery of a contemporary industrial, and even more, a warring world. The human and the inhuman have been fused.

For Smith, his materials have symbolic importance: they evoke the power, the speed, the destructiveness of modern technology. As its title indicates, *Tank Totem* V combines the supposed rationality of contemporary culture with the presumed irrationality of the primitive. It unites a visually clear and rhythmic formal structure—by itself invigorating—with the menace of intimidating force.

Multiple reference plays an analogous role in Lipton's *Sea King* where the flow of space around and into the open, indented parts reveals the continuing constructivist tradition, put to the uses of symbolism. However modified and abstract, this is an organic creature of some sort, suggesting at once fish and crustacean. There is a quite deliberate discrepancy between the jagged, broken elements and the smoothly joined forms to which they allude. To a large degree this tension is achieved through the exploitation of modern materials. Soft metals brazed onto a strong sheet of hard metal produce a surface of vary-

left
Robert Müller
Aaron's Rod. 1958

opposite
Herbert Ferber
Calligraph with Sloping Roof, One Wall II
1957–61

ing textural and color effects. The hollow, space-defining forms, conceived as joined shells are made possible by the strength of modern alloys. The original conceptual "purity" of the constructivist ideal has thus been doubly modified: by a richness of materials whose sparkle catches the eye, and by the reintroduction of natural objects. The result is a romantic metaphor employed with a symbolic intention.

The mechanical and the organic are once more brought together in Müller's *Aaron's Rod.* The first impact is of a built-up construction, of the darkness of its light-absorbing surface, and the strength of its separate forms and broken silhouette: an abstract, vertically balanced composition. Only gradually does one become aware that its bulbous shapes, leaf forms, and shoots derive from, or are contained in, its theme and suggest sprouting growth. Its somber material, iron instead of the more conventionally attractive bronze, contrasts with the hopeful expectancy of the subject, giving it an allusive intensity. In the same way a naturally continuous growth is translated into interrupted, pointed forms put together of separate pieces of bent metal, each with its own character. Surprisingly, these independent shapes are close to their naturalistic source. It is this fusion, achieved with no loss of identity to either abstraction or naturalistic reference, which is the artist's aim.

The representational sources of Nakian's *Olympia,* although more hidden than Müller's, are equally pervasive. But they are of a different order. Nakian starts not from nature, but from art. Nearly abstract though the work is, its title suggests its classic beginnings. The clue to Nakian's inspiration in Greek pediment figures lies in his freestanding but frontal design; he too spreads out parts and avoids overlapping and foreshortening. The extended leg, the frontally turned torso and shoulder, the

bent arm, which so often occur in pediment compositions, have become so stylized that they are more sensed than represented. Yet they inform proportion and relation, restraining the expressionist tone of the rough surface and jagged silhouette, conflicting qualities that are joined in a tragic intensity.

The examples of expressionist constructivism so far illustrated have all modified the original principle of abstract space-shaping through allusion to objects. But the expressionist tendency can also function through its own kind of abstraction. Ferber's *Calligraph with Sloping Roof, One Wall II* sets up a room-like space, an architectural interior seen as a unit from outside. Inside, like a vigorous gesture, confined yet free, moves a heavy metal line. This is three-dimensional drawing, but it differs in two ways from what has been called space drawing. First, it is traced within an already established volume, which it divides and apportions, rather than defining that volume itself (compare Giacometti's *Palace at 4 A.M.*, page 75); and second, this irregular and perhaps angry line is determined by immediate intuition rather than analytic reflection (compare Lippold's *Variation Number 7: Full Moon,* page 78). Such a work is the counterpart of New York School abstract expressionism.

Because constructivist sculpture (whether geometrical or expressionist in emphasis) aims at clear and evident spatial configuration, it has affinities with architecture, which also composes space. But architectural space is actual—it can be entered and used; sculptural space is virtual—it remains external and abstract, grasped through the eye alone. Since we observe it from the outside, its flow and movement affect us by analogy. Understandably, the modern sculptor is often tempted to approach architecture. When he does, as in Étienne-Martin's *Demeure 3,* he builds a symbolic (not a functional) dwelling, useful to the

Reuben Nakian
Olympia. 1961

spirit alone. Though we walk through this construction, we do so as spectators, and though we enter its walls, it remains open while it surrounds us. Its many and different chambers, arranged in rock-like formation, or as an irregular honeycomb, recall some primitive village shelter, part natural, part man-made habitation. The interiors of this symbolic pueblo offer us a visual and therefore an emotional refuge.

Henri Étienne-Martin
Demeure 3. 1960

Assemblage

Sculpture's traditional materials have been stone, wood, clay, and bronze; its techniques have been carving and modeling. All these have been continued by modern sculptors, but others have been added. Constructivism, seeking to make space perceptible, found new means by which to compose the new materials of an industrial technology. Assemblage is equally untraditional, but it is its attitudes, not its skills, that make it contemporary. Its varying results are produced by one essential method: the bringing together (assembling) rather than the making (creating) of the work's constituent parts. As the work grows, the artist responds, shifting, adjusting, regrouping by a subjective process of sensitive organization. In its ideal definition, assemblage uses as its elements only pre-existent objects (natural or fabricated—but not by the artist), which it combines into a new whole. As in collage, from which sculptural assemblage grew, creation lies less in the skills of craftsmanship than in the power of imagination. But in practice the sculptor usually both finds and makes the forms he assembles into a unity. In practice, too, assemblage has tended to employ used objects rather than new ones, objects whose personal history has furnished them with an identity. And within a single work it has often mixed its materials, deliberately provoking unfamiliar association. Primacy of the imagination, and juxtapositions which both prompt and manifest that imagination—these are surrealist principles which have affected assemblage only to the extent to which they have generally influenced all of modern art.

The subject matter of Picasso's *Still Life* is characteristically cubist: the utensils and the food and drink that go to make up a studio lunch are all familiar from his paintings. So

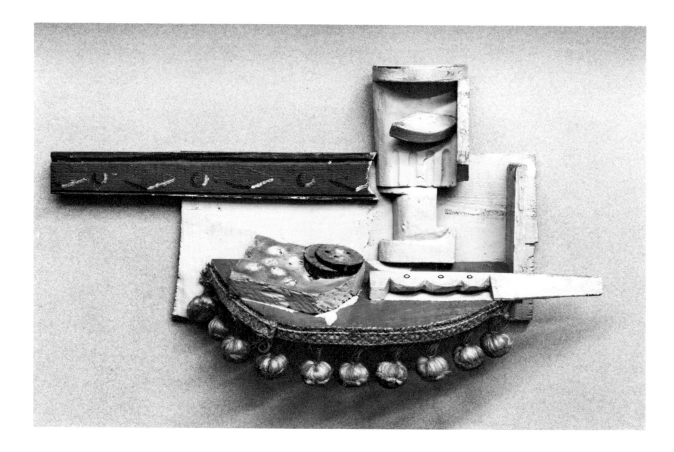

Pablo Picasso
Still Life. 1914

left
Kurt Schwitters
Merz Construction. 1921

opposite
Joan Miró
Poetic Object. 1936

too is the fusion of two perspectives (horizontal and vertical) into a single view, and the cutting away of the glass in order to spell out all the known parts of a carefully balanced composition which fades off at the edges. Wooden objects and others are all imitated in wood, and then artificially painted to make them look more real; and an upholstery fringe is added. Picasso thus questions the nature of artistic illusion, just as his rough carpentry puts in doubt the use of artistic skill, and his deft but candid representation comments ironically on artistic pomposity.

If *Still Life* foreshadows dada by suggesting that art can be made out of anything, Schwitters's *Merz Construction* is this idea's deliberate demonstration. Assembled here are old wood, wire mesh, paper, cardboard, and other materials—a gathering of castoff fragments. As found, they were doubly worthless: worn out, and no longer functionally useful; without design, and so to the ordinary eye no longer aesthetically useful. Reassembled by Schwitters, they now have a new dignity—they have become worth looking at. Through order, proportion, and balanced areas, through interlocking outlines and contrasts of color and texture, each old element of this essentially cubist composition has been given a new life. Schwitters's rejection of accepted techniques and artistic values was programmatic in origin (reflecting a social critique), but its execution rested upon an acute and flexible sensitivity to hitherto unnoticed visual qualities of despised materials. For him, their rehabilitation had profound moral implications.

Because they are composed of fragments and not of objects, Schwitters's assemblages (despite their philosophic base in dada) appear to us as abstract compositions following cubist principles. The title of Miró's *Poetic Object* suggests its very different intention. Its logic is that of surrealism, the unpredictable logic

96

of the imagination, which discovers, as in dreams, that chance meetings are not haphazard and can reveal unsuspected meanings. One could elaborate an iconography for this strange assemblage: man (hat) and woman (leg), earth (map) and sky (bird), but it would be undemonstrable. And it is unnecessary, since the whole captures the imagination and arouses wonder. Nevertheless, our response is by no means caused only by the objects so surprisingly juxtaposed. Miró has also known how to balance dark and light and suggest the immensity of open space.

Though the techniques of assemblage were at first employed by painters as an extension of collage, by 1950 sculptors made assemblage their own, and it has since been effectively used for its inherent possibilities. Bourgeois's *Quarantania, I* takes the method of assemblage at its most literal. Each of its wooden elements, painted white or blue, is a separate unit anchored in a base that serves as common ground for a concentrated gathering of carved abstract shapes. Similar but not identical, their rhythms and relations give the work its formal interest. At the same time, as the attenuated, organic curves suggest, there is a symbolic reference. Here is a human group, its members alike but various, leaning toward one another in an intensity of feeling that unites them even as it leaves each one silent and alone.

The human reference in Stankiewicz's *Instruction* is more explicit despite its machine parts, but its tone is ironic. There is admonition in the larger cylinder which, with a rhetorical gesture, addresses the squat and docile figure on the right. The humor resides in the double identity of the parts, since for all their clear human suggestion they retain the integrity of their mechanical origins. Unlike the parts of Picasso's *Bull's Head* (page 53), of which they are the distant descendants, the

opposite
Louise Bourgeois
Quarantania, I. 1948–53

above
Richard Stankiewicz
Instruction. 1957

"found objects" from which this group is assembled are never completely fused into a new image. The tension between what they once were and what they now are remains essential. Yet Stankiewicz is aware that (as with Schwitters's *Merz Construction*) time and familiarity may dull the ironic edge. "The only thing," he says, "that can make a sculpture a legitimately interesting object, quite apart from whatever message it may or may not have, is the discipline of organization." In other words, such a work is heir to both dada and abstraction.

Violence, not delicacy, dominates Chamberlain's use of industrial debris in his untitled composition. Strong and sudden forces seem to have bent these metal sheets, now twisted and torn into cavernous and macabre forms. The spontaneous movement of abstract expressionist painting, its impetuous overlapping brush strokes and brilliant color planes, are here translated into metal. The work's immediate power lies in its expression of a seemingly undirected energy, a kind of playful fury. The associations with violent, real-life accident are inevitable—and intentional—although they are softened by the attractive colors. But after the initial impact, they hold the attention only because of the abstract "discipline of organization."

Pure physical size is also important to di Suvero's *Pre-Columbian*. Its many materials—driftwood, old iron pipes and beams, a rubber tire—used for their varying textures and their romantic associations of discard and weathering, imply revolt against society's organized efficiency. They tell us that here is a sculptural beachcomber, living only on what comes to hand. In these respects, di Suvero's assemblage is an intensification of dada, but its style (to which large scale is essential) is of a later time. Its open composition through which space flows, its strongly linear elements cross-

opposite
Mark di Suvero
Pre-Columbian. 1965

above
John Chamberlain
Untitled. 1960

99

ing at sharp angles, its concentrated blacks massed against uneven whites, all these reveal the proximity of abstract expressionism, whose irregular edges and drips seem here to have their wooden counterparts. To swing in the tire (as one can) is only to activate the work's powerfully suggested movement.

Any assemblage of worn, discarded objects protests against accepted definitions of art. But, once used, they are themselves gradually accepted, and their original purpose is lost in a new aesthetic, with its own conventions. But the "anti-art" impulse can find more radical ways to startle the observer into new realizations; it can attack the desire for permanence basic to the creation of most painting and sculpture. "Resist the anxious fear to fix the instantaneous, to kill that which is living," Tinguely has said. *Eureka* is a demonstration of this resistance. It exists only temporarily in this handsome static form; if set in motion it would proceed to its own destruction. It is a pseudomachine whose only function is to appear to function. Its impressive appearance, which is its only reality, gives it an ironic existence as a work of art.

Jean Tinguely
Eureka. 1964

Tendencies of the Sixties

Sculpture in the mid-sixties developed in two broadly contrasting directions. On the one hand the abstract tradition, still dominant, moved toward a reduction of the number and complication of its parts, employing simplification in the interests of intensity. On the other, there was a revival of several kinds of realism in which naturalistic detail was either viewed neutrally and composed as abstraction or was put to the service of social commentary, serious or satirical.

The elements of David Smith's *Cubi* X at first appear to be nothing more than rectangles and squares—shallow geometric volumes (they are hollow) that barely touch one another and are cantilevered into space. Yet this is not an entirely abstract composition. Its three-part division, slender at the bottom, then widening and narrowing again, and its clearly marked central axis with projecting arms are based on memories of the human form—now simplified. And the frontality of its elements, the way they intersect and overlap, the buffing that modulates the bright planes, all these stem ultimately from cubism—now made more abstract and monumental. For Smith the polish of the stainless steel was essential: "I have used atmosphere," he said, "in a reflective way on the surfaces. They are colored by the sky and the surroundings."

The roots of kinetic sculpture may be found in earlier constructivism, for which both a spatial continuum and the idea of movement through space were basic concepts. But there motion was almost always ideal, more implied than actual. Rickey's *Two Lines* envisions movement at the work's inception, and does so with calculated and mathematical efficiency. Exactitude is essential to the precise balances that produce repetition and satisfy

David Smith
Cubi X. 1963

opposite
George Rickey
Two Lines—Temporal I. 1964

above
Anthony Caro
Sculpture Two. 1962

the expectancy of recurrent rhythms. (Calder's apparent spontaneity of invention and adjustment contrasts with this more "scientific" method of analysis. Compare page 76.) It is basic to kinetic sculpture that it make evident the rational interdependence of its parts and the measurable development of the changing spatial intervals they create.

Caro's extended openwork *Sculpture Two* inherits aspects of both constructivism and assemblage. It puts together everyday structural units. The heavy beams are painted "to render their massive substance largely optical," that is, having the least possible sense of weight. "I don't compose," Caro has said, "I put them up the way I want them and see them later . . . my decisions . . . are not compositional decisions." (Compare the di Suvero, page 98.) This intention is emphasized by the way the work stretches out along the ground and through the space of the spectator's actual experience. Thus random placing, casual handling, and color all deny the actual tonnage of the material.

Literal space, and the transformation of "object" into "art," are also essential to Tony Smith's *Cigarette*. The "paced unfolding of form" which Smith conceives as "interruptions in an otherwise unbroken flow of space" places a double emphasis on volume. The somewhat awkward black shapes are hollow, thus enclosing space within themselves; and one must walk through and around them to grasp their relationships. Although they seem to sprawl and stretch they also push against each other, and their geometric twisting is both careless and ominous. The scale, the roughness, the lack of detail are all part of Smith's desire to avoid the "intimacy and sensuousness" of previous sculpture, and to create instead an "awareness of oneself as existing in the same space as the work. . . . The object itself has not become less important, it has become less self-important."

Tony Smith
Cigarette. 1967

opposite
Ronald Bladen
Untitled. 1966–67

above
Donald Judd
Untitled. 1965

Bladen's untitled construction is similar in several ways: the three rhomboids are hollow (weights keep them upright), larger than man-size, and painted black. Bladen also starts with repeated (modular) units, modified as intuition dictates. But while the simplicity of the units and the arrangement of the work stress its conceptual origin, it is more easily grasped visually. The isolation of the elements, their repetition, and relation all are effective from a distance. The emphasis is on the planar surfaces; scale, shape, sequence, and interval in precise adjustment are all crucial. As in much modern painting, simplification in one direction demands and permits increased awareness in others. Bladen has said that his purpose is to achieve "more drama as a result of . . . reduction. . . . What I am after is to create a drama out of a minimal experience."

It is precisely this kind of drama that Judd wishes to remove from his work. By employing the simplest forms, mechanically manufactured from predetermined modular specifications, he aims at a "form of neutrality." Thus removed from its subjective origin, the work will be seen as impersonal, existing entirely in its own right and attaining a maximum "identity as object," free of creative contingency. This is an extreme of structuralism, an invention so conceptual and at the same time so literal in its acceptance of material fact that the work "becomes dominated by its own means." It is a thing among other things, whose "thingness" questions the nature of art.

These works are all "abstract," yet they share a common "realistic" purpose: to create and shape, to immerse the spectator actively in, and heighten his awareness of, an immediate "real" environment.

Representation as it is usually understood (rather than presentation) is the starting point of Segal's *Woman Shaving Her Legs*. This is a contemporary genre subject which, by com-

opposite
George Segal
Woman Shaving Her Legs. 1963

above
Jean Ipousteguy
Alexander before Ecbatane. 1965

pletely accepting its realistic premise, by-passes traditional skills of imitation. The figure is a plaster cast made in sections over a living model, its setting an actual bathtub complete with fixtures and wall tile, and the whole is thus in its own way "environmental." But the figure, stark white, over life-size, its features rough and generalized, is the very opposite of natural. It combines, but does not reconcile, the instantaneous and the eternal, change and immobility (in contrast to Degas, page 30). Moreover, this is a carefully spaced-out composition in high relief. Segal uses the realistic figure to create an awareness of the "peculiar shape and qualities of the actual empty air surrounding the volumes." (Compare Nicholson's *Painted Relief*, page 118.)

Ipousteguy's subject is conventionally heroic, its treatment is not. *Alexander before Ecbatane* is on the verge of conquests that will lead him to India, and to his death. This is the moment of temptation, of the vision of power and plunder that will end in tragedy. The heroism lies in the force of the large, block-like figure, its dramatic gestures, the vitality of its glance; but it is a heroism overblown by its own conceit. The fixed eyes are really blind, seeing only their own desires; self-absorption splits the skull; the hero has become a robot, driven into compulsive action across the land that lies before him. Ipousteguy has conceived a symbol of the self-destruction that dooms the conqueror; and its antique subject disguises a modern morality.

Paolozzi's *Hermaphroditic Idol Number 1* has no likeness to anything but itself, yet it has its own nightmare realism. It correctly materializes a vision we have never seen but immediately recognize. As in Goya's dream of reason that produces monsters, Paolozzi has confronted what he has called the "rational order of the technological world" and by pushing its image to a logical conclusion has pro-

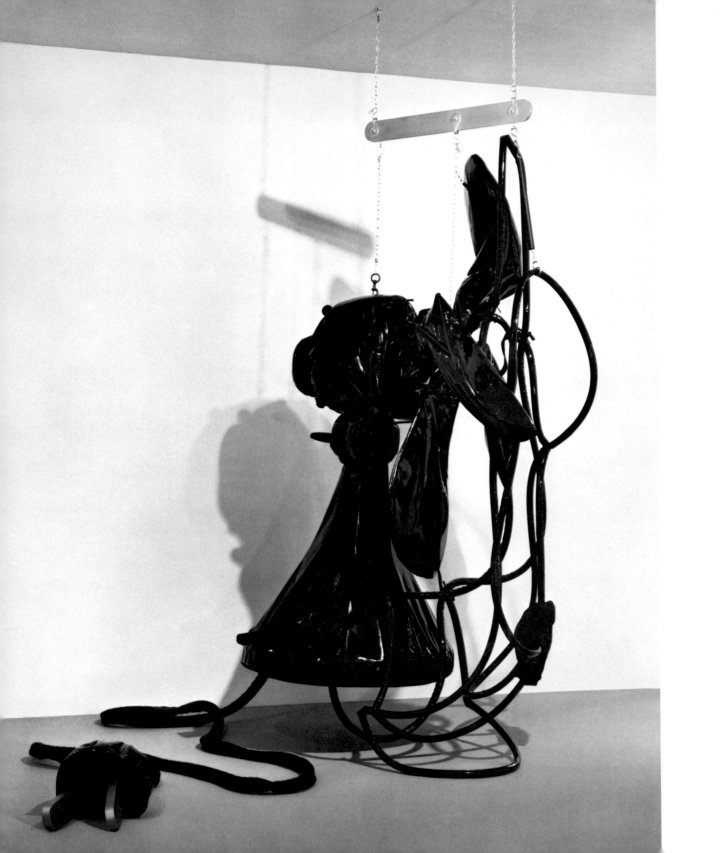

duced an irrational mechanical fetish. It is a construction with vaguely human features, a nonfunctioning machine brought into existence only by man's desire to worship his own inventions. It is a symbol of a computerized self-multiplying world from which nature has been excluded and in which man no longer dares to intervene.

The machine world also fascinates Oldenburg, but it does not terrify him. Because we are concerned only with their immediate use, its products (the manufactured landscape we live in) remain unseen and the magic they contain, unfelt. Oldenburg wants to restore this consciousness. In *Giant Soft Fan* he remakes a familiar object out of an unexpected and functionally impossible material. Its stuffed softness has changed its structure, scale, and character, and made us suddenly aware of both this fan and all those fans to which we usually are blind. Oldenburg says he uses "naive imitation . . . to create an independent object." "I want people to get accustomed to recognize the power of objects. . . . I alter to unfold the object and to add to it other object-qualities. . . ." Such transformations perhaps contain an implicit social commentary, but the artist's conscious primary concern is with formal metamorphosis.

opposite
Claes Oldenburg
Giant Soft Fan. 1966–67

above
Eduardo Paolozzi
Hermaphroditic Idol Number 1. 1962

Relief

Sculptural reliefs, in the past, have generally been tied to an architectural setting. The sculptor has been called upon to create a work for a particular, predetermined spot, and asked to make it fit in appearance and spirit. Usually his subject has been decided for him. The modern sculptor has rarely been employed in this fashion. Patrons, especially public patrons (corporate, civic, or religious) have been timid, and recent architecture widely committed to a tradition of ascetic undecorated surface, whose effect sculpture would only mar. For these reasons most of the relief sculpture of this century, like most of its freestanding sculpture, has been the product of the artist's free and independent invention, unconditioned by the specific requirements of a client or a commission. It is thus natural that relief sculpture should share in the explorations and development of sculpture as a whole. Created by the same artists, its limitation to two dimensions has been self-imposed.

In Maillol's composition, *Desire*, for example, we recognize his concentration on the classic nude, with tradition further reinforced by a deliberate reminiscence of the mythological struggles depicted on ancient Doric metopes. Like those of the Parthenon, the figures fill out the four sides of the square. The result is a theme of balanced, arrested action, the more intense for being so rigidly confined.

Although rhythmically designed, and generalized, Maillol's figures still have all the stresses and strains of naturalism. Duchamp-Villon's *Lovers* stylizes the same theme into a more abstract language, partly cubist, partly futurist. The equal emphasis given to projection and recession (that is, to figure and to background), with its overall patterning of light and dark and the answering oval shapes,

114

above
Raymond Duchamp-Villon
The Lovers. 1913

opposite
Aristide Maillol
Desire. 1906–8

left
Henri Matisse
The Back, IV. 1929?

opposite
Jean Arp
Relief. 1938–39

is in the cubist mode; the sense of movement given by the taut, drawn-out contours and flame-like forms stems from futurism.

The sense of a form-controlling design is strong in both these compositions. Matisse's even greater stylization in *The Back, IV* suggests no such external restraints. It is the last of an increasingly simplified series that progresses from a relatively detailed naturalism toward this broad, powerful interpretation. Here the figure has been reduced to essentials, yet the effect is not of limitation but of growth, as if its structure, coalescing out of the undifferentiated mass, was momentarily arrested at this point, its humanity just visible but still one with the inanimate material. In this respect it is related to Rodin's *Dance Movement D* (page 32).

Equally abstract, equally sustained by the limits of a single consistent kind of form, the reliefs of Arp and Nicholson are nevertheless based on very different premises. The difference goes deeper than the clear contrast of irregular and geometric shapes. Nicholson's *Painted Relief* is within the tradition of carefully deliberated, finely studied abstraction best known in the paintings of Mondrian; it is founded on the exact adjustment and conscious control of a small number of "pure" forms. Arp, on the other hand, shares the dada faith in inspiration and accident; his forms are "free" and each one is unique; their relations and their intervals submit to no laws and can be based upon chance or sudden discovery. Thus one is "classic," the other "romantic." Nevertheless, both ultimately rely on the workings of a fine sensibility, sharpened by a long concentration on a narrow range of formal elements, which accepts (or rejects) what is proposed by the conscious "rules" or by unconscious "chance."

Each compartment of Nevelson's *Sky Cathedral*, framed in a box, is composed in a

above
Ben Nicholson
Painted Relief. 1939

opposite
Louise Nevelson
Sky Cathedral. 1958
118

119

above
Constantino Nivola
Freestanding Mural. 1964

opposite
Pietro Consagra
Conversation before the Mirror. 1957

cubist vocabulary of harmoniously overlapping curvilinear and straight silhouettes. Made up of castoff bits of carpentry, each unit, like the relief as a whole, is an assemblage. But unlike the re-used objects of earlier collage, these elements were already "artistic," nostalgic pieces of a valued folk aesthetic, and so reassuring rather than ironically disturbing. Color and size are effective contrasts to these bohemian constituents: multiplication gives them emphasis, unexpected blackness binds them into a muted, brooding whole.

These various but related traditions seem fused in Nivola's much larger *Freestanding Mural.* Its alternating relief and recession, its interlocking curved and angled patterns are grounded in an earlier cubism, as are its restrained harmonies. But there is a relaxation of detail and surface, an exploitation of toughness and accident, and a size that are in the spirit of a later, less calculated style. In a manner Le Corbusier first used effectively for his architecture, the imperfections of the molds in which the cement was cast have been allowed to remain, thus emphasizing that, resistant to the artist's will, the work has its own material character.

Such accidents, only partially controlled, and such materiality, play an even more determining role in Consagra's *Conversation before the Mirror.* This is also a freestanding relief, cast from laminated wood. The uneven indentations that animate the surface owe their shapes to the irregular splitting of the original material, a characteristic the sculptor has knowingly exploited. He has thus achieved the quality of apparent accident and seemingly natural damage that at the same time enhances the surface. Its expressionist effect is comparable to that of César's *Torso* (page 16).

Despite their greater freedom, these more recent reliefs share with the Arp and the Nicholson a certain consistency and cleanliness in

their material substance. These are purposely denied in Mallary's *In Flight*. Like di Suvero's assemblage (page 98), which it also resembles in its open composition, it calls attention to the ordinary unaesthetic character of its constituent debris. We can admire its texture, interval, and contrast in a casual and subtle organization of elements, now separated from any previous use. As in the earlier practice of Schwitters, deliberate poverty of material thus enhances the richness of formal structure (page 94). But by now such nonaesthetic simplicity has become an accepted aesthetic quality and, with the initial critical intention forgotten, it can be used directly for a romantic theme.

Purely technically, Bontecou's strongly projecting untitled relief is made like an assemblage, since it is sewn together out of pieces of burlap scrap. But assemblage is usually flexible and impressionist in attitude, responding and giving in to its materials, whereas this somewhat violent construction is a determined conception willed onto strained and reluctant elements. Its glue-stretched membranes pull stiff against their barbed, wire seams (the pliable forced into rigidity), and a crater's void is sunk into the center of a volcano-like design.

opposite
Lee Bontecou
Untitled. 1960

above
Robert Mallary
In Flight. 1957

Monuments

Most modern painting and sculpture is created through the artist's "inner necessity" and in accordance with his own individual concept. He judges it satisfactory when it comes near to meeting the ideals of form and expression he has set for himself. Approval comes afterward, if at all. The artist wants his audience to meet him on his own terms, and he takes account of its tastes and demands only in an indirect and usually unconscious fashion. Outside himself only his fellow artists set standards he respects.

This tradition is one important reason why modern sculptural monuments are rare. They require previous agreement on the part of artist and client, and this is difficult. Only the famous artist will be allowed a free hand, and even then his work may be refused, as was Rodin's *Monument to Balzac* (page 35). But creative individualism is only one of many problems. It is part of the same changing context that has made for the erosion of the accepted, meaningful civic and religious symbols of the past. Thus for monumental sculpture too the artist has had to rely almost entirely upon himself for an effective theme and form; any adaptation to purpose and site can result only from his free decision. The work of some artists is by its very nature more suitable to the large scale necessary for an effective monumental form, and this requirement has been automatically selective. Nevertheless, in general, monumental works have been as varied as modern sculpture itself.

Thus Barlach's *Güstrow War Memorial* employs his mystic medievalizing style virtually unchanged. Although in bronze, and much larger than his usual wooden figures, this hovering angel is modeled in the same broad planes, has the same peasant head, and

opposite
Reg Butler
The Unknown Political Prisoner. 1951–53

above
Ernst Barlach
Güstrow War Memorial. 1926

carries the same trance-like intensity of feel-ing. The unexpected floating form, seemingly borne upward by the rising movement of the vertical church space, is a remarkably effec-tive spiritual symbol, whose pathos is suffused with faith.

Also a memorial, but belonging to a later time and dedicated to the victims of another war, Butler's *The Unknown Political Prisoner (Project for a Monument)* inevitably has a dif-ferent character. Conceived in the construc-tivist mode, it is open, and at first sight abstract, with a free-flowing space playing a predominant role. Only gradually do the sin-ister associations of the linear design become apparent. Its stabbing, encircling wires recall the electrified barriers of the concentration camp; its figures are dwarfed by the overpow-ering mechanical contrivance whose delicacy intensifies its menace. Where Barlach tran-scends mortality through faith, and expresses that faith in an enlarged naturalism, Butler, confining his minute, isolated figures on a rocky ledge, points to an individual despairing bravery, sustained by a common humanity. It is perhaps ironically fitting that this monument to unrecognized heroism was never built.

Like Barlach, Moore, in his *King and Queen*, deliberately invokes the dignifying memories of past styles. Barlach's associations are Gothic and religious; Moore's are classic, secular, and primitivizing. His gaunt figures and geometricized heads are related to sur-realist stylizations (compare Ernst, page 55), and like them have been inspired by early Mediterranean sculpture. The royal couple also refers to classic tragedy and to the tradi-tion of English landscape sentiment. The bare ground these figures dominate, the lighted sky around them, and the infinite distances their gazes suggest are all essential to Moore's con-cept. For all its Cycladic simplicity this is a romantic monument, using both nature and

Henry Moore
King and Queen. 1952–53

above
Antoine Pevsner
Bird Flight. 1955–56

opposite
Pablo Picasso
The Bathers. 1956

man's ancient history to celebrate his moral grandeur and loneliness.

While such seriousness is essential to Moore, it would seem pretentious to Picasso. His *Bathers* are companionable and humorous, gay rather than dour, playful rather than austere, and above all not sublime. They are at home only in a trimmed and civilized nature, with measurable distances. The group's rectangular framework heightens its inner relationships. The stylization of its figures refers less to past eras (as with Moore) than to Picasso's own history, since this work, done in the fifties, develops the geometric simplifications that he and González had begun more than twenty

years earlier (compare page 74). This comment on his own art, characteristic for Picasso, amplifies the humor of the shorthand references to nature which give each figure its own distinct personality.

At first sight Pevsner's *Bird Flight* and Noguchi's *Sunken Courtyard* are monuments of the same kind: both seem to employ the language of nonrepresentational form. In fact, they are as symbolic as they are abstract, and complement and contrast with each other. One rises as a vertical from the horizontal surface of an artificial plain so large that it resembles a natural plateau; the other—"a landscape of the imagination"—is set into the "cloistered containment" of a sunken courtyard and all its elements are kept low. Pevsner's thrusting form is of metal, the material of the surrounding factory complex and of the cars the company makes. Noguchi's court is entirely of traditional marble, like the translucent windowless walls of the adjacent library of rare books. It is a monument not to movement and modernity like Pevsner's, but to continuity and the wisdom of the past, not to activity, but to contemplation. Thus Pevsner, following constructivist principles, brings space into a composition whose presence also organizes and controls the surrounding space, and recalls the romantic symbol of the soaring bird. Noguchi, fusing eastern and western traditions, employs philosophic signs: the pyramid for the earth (or matter), the circle for the sun (or energy), and the cube, a balanced die, for chance (or the human condition).

Isamu Noguchi
Sunken Courtyard. 1960–64

Architecture as Sculpture

Architecture's first task would seem to be to provide shelter—that is, protected interior space. The space needed may be minimal (as in a tomb) or it may be vast (as in a sports arena), and so the relation of mass to void is infinitely variable. Similarly exterior and interior shape (the covering and the covered) may be in close conformity, so that appearance anticipates entrance, or relatively independent, so that the interior space surprises by its contraction or expansion. These relations—mass to void, surface to volume, skin to skeleton—are also fundamental to sculpture, and thus all architecture is in some measure sculptural.

Two factors have brought modern architecture and sculpture into a more conscious relationship. Since a large portion of recent sculpture has been nonfigurative it has had to confront more directly than in the past the harmonious reconciliation of abstract forms and spaces which have been the architect's traditional concern. The architect, in return, through the modern materials of glass, steel, concrete, and plastic can have a command of space and a freedom of form akin to that assumed by the sculptor. Some modern architects have been aware of these potentialities, and some modern architecture has been markedly "sculptural" in aspect and in spirit.

Rodin's *Model for a Monument to Labor* and Tatlin's *Model for a Monument for the Third International* are the architectural concepts of sculptors; neither was ever executed at full scale. Although separated by nearly a quarter of a century they are related in both theme and expression. Rodin's project is still tied to traditional forms (and materials) of mausoleum, monument, and heroic sculpture, imaginatively combined if not fused. Its exceptional open structure and sense of move-

opposite
Auguste Rodin
Model for a Monument to Labor. 1894

right
Vladimir Tatlin
Model for a Monument for the Third International. 1920

ment into space, its vigorous alternation of light and shade (the hollow and the lump on a magnified scale), its use of the tensions of imbalance, all these grow out of Rodin's sculptural concerns.

Tatlin's spiral "tower" has renounced the past. The use of the latest industrial technology has permitted an open, space-penetrated design, the relation of whose parts in a changing three-dimensional rhythm is clearly visible. As in constructivist sculpture mass is eliminated (or as nearly as stability will allow) and planes become the delimitation of space whose measure is depth. But where Gabo insisted upon purity, Tatlin's monument was conceived as "the resolution of the most difficult problem of culture, that of unifying utilitarian and purely creative form." The spiral framework enclosed four glass-walled rotating chambers devoted to the activities of government. Thus projected in both use and structure into the surrounding space, this functional monument, to be constructed of obviously modern materials, symbolized the optimism of the moment—the harmonious mastery of his environment that would ensure man's happy, humane future.

Tatlin's continuous spiral contrasts with Rietveld's design of interlocking rectangles. Here there are no curves, but only straight lines and right angles, whether in the planes or where they meet. The transparent rectangles formed by windows, doors, and railings are as important to the design as the opaque panels of the walls, and the horizontal projections of roofs and balconies as essential as their vertically suspended counterparts. There is no single axis or center of attention but an equally distributed emphasis on each of the intersecting, asymmetric, balanced units. If this design, which carries to the edges and beyond, is something like the sculptural development of a canvas by Mondrian, it is be-

Gerrit Rietveld
Schröder House. 1924

135

cause Rietveld shared the philosophy of the De Stijl group. For them, horizontal and vertical were fundamental units of the ideal (but only truly real) universe usually concealed beneath the accidents of appearance. The task of the artist (architect or painter) was to reveal its hidden structure.

For Tatlin and Rietveld the evidence of construction is crucial; they compose their materials (different as these are) so that it will remain apparent. Gaudí has no interest in this kind of "truth to materials." His Casa Milá has a softly sculptural surface that seems to have been modeled in clay before it was cast in concrete and that conceals its method of support. The polygonal facade has no one orientation; lintels and cornices are curved, uprights vary in diameter, vertical flows into horizontal, windows seem to have been pushed through the thick malleable material of the wall. Its continuous undulation is heightened by the bands wrapped around it to divide the stories. Gaudí belongs to the time of art nouveau, but he has handled its usually flat, decorative line in three dimensions, as a sculptor would. Yet for all its freedom of modeling Gaudí's building (unlike most art nouveau) is heavy, mysterious, closed in upon itself.

The curved concrete shapes of Mendelsohn's Einstein Tower have greater sweep and direction. From the angled enclosure of the entrance steps through the horizontal base that rises into the thrust of the tower this is a purposeful architecture—solid, energetic support for the telescopic dome. The squat windows let into the thick walls are sudden, dark contrasts against the bright, taut, unbroken outer surfaces. The tower seems a fortress of modern science, at once functional and intense, produced by the same positive faith as Tatlin's *Monument*. Although this is an expressionist architecture it has the cleanness of design and, in its details, the combi-

opposite
Antoni Gaudí
Casa Milá. 1905–7

above
Eric Mendelsohn
Einstein Tower. 1920–21

nation of straight and curved lines of the post-cubist twenties.

Even larger in its sweep and simplicity, Le Corbusier's chapel at Ronchamp has a much bolder freedom. Its three elements, the curved walls meeting like a ship's prow, the white tower, and the rolled overhanging roof all seem free of the problems of structure and stability, conceived for their formal and expressive contrast alone. Window openings follow no axial lines. Shadow and light are in such strong contrast as to have the effect of color. The forms Le Corbusier uses here belong to the same family as the biomorphic shapes of Arp and Moore, having the same tension, the same union of the geometric and the organic. They are made possible by the properties of reinforced concrete, handled with a sculptor's sense of overall proportion and design. The freedom is such that the exterior hardly suggests the interior. Although this is in fact a closed and isolated space, with something of the concentration of a Romanesque interior, it opens out (somewhat like a Calder, page 62) to embrace light and sky.

The free forms made feasible by modern materials have been further exploited by Saarinen in his TWA Terminal. The prestressed concrete arcs, anchored by thin wedges, rise from a low center and soar outward toward clear end surfaces without external supports. They pull against one another, held not by traditional resistance to compression, but by the tensile strength within the material. This force is perceived in the stretched character of the curves, which are seen as mechanical wings related to the building's airport function. These forms are no mere automatic outcome of utilitarian purpose or materials; they were the initial imaginative concept. But their interaction has been heightened and dramatized, and through the interior play of light and shade and the silhouette

opposite
Le Corbusier
Notre Dame du Haut. 1950–54

above
Eero Saarinen
TWA Terminal. 1957–62

against the sky they have become the symbols of flight.

Material and function have more direct results in Lundy's Exhibition Building. It is air pressure against a double nylon skin that produces these smooth domed forms resting gently on the ground like worn marble hills. Sculpturally these closed forms, at once abstract and bulbously organic, similar in their effect to some of Brancusi's and Arp's, are more traditional than those of previous architecture. But now the scale is immense, and the interior space paradoxically more open and uninterrupted than any other structural system would allow. And no more here than elsewhere is there an inevitable technological determination. Engineering permits a certain number of solutions, and new demands and new materials widen the range of the architect's artistic choices.

Victor A. Lundy
Inflatable Exhibition Building
for the Atomic Energy Commission
1960–63

Artists and Sculptures

Artists' names are arranged alphabetically; their works are listed chronologically. In the dimensions height precedes width; for some works a third dimension, depth, is given; for others only height or length is given. Page numbers refer to illustrations.

Alexander Archipenko
American. Born 1887, Kiev, Russia. Worked in Paris 1908–21; to United States, 1923. Died in New York, 1964.

Struggle (Boxing). 1914. Bronze, 23¼ x 18¼ x 16⅞". The Museum of Modern Art, New York. Gift of Donald H. Karshan. *Page 51*
Woman Combing Her Hair. 1915. Bronze, 13¾" high. The Museum of Modern Art, New York. Acquired through the Lillie P. Bliss Bequest. *Page 43*

Jean (Hans) Arp
French. Born 1887, Strasbourg (then Germany). Settled in Meudon (near Paris), 1926; to Switzerland, 1942. Died in Basel, 1966.

Human Concretion. 1935. Original plaster, 19½ x 18¾". The Museum of Modern Art, New York. Gift of the Advisory Committee. *Page 60*
Relief. 1938–39, after a relief of 1934–35. Wood, 19½ x 19⅝". The Museum of Modern Art, New York. Gift of the Advisory Committee (by exchange). *Page 117*

Ernst Barlach
German. Born 1870, Wedel (near Hamburg). Lived in Güstrow. Died in Rostock, 1938.

Man Drawing a Sword. 1911. Wood, 31" high. Galleries—Cranbrook Academy of Art, Bloomfield Hills, Michigan. *Page 40*
Güstrow War Memorial. 1926. Bronze, 7'7" long. Antoniterkirche, Cologne. *Page 125*

Rudolf Belling
German. Born 1886, Berlin. In Istanbul, 1937–65. Lives near Munich.

Sculpture. 1923. Bronze, partly silvered, 18⅞ x 7¾ x 8½". The Museum of Modern Art, New York. A. Conger Goodyear Fund. *Page 46*

Ronald Bladen
American. Born 1918, Vancouver, British Columbia. Lives in New York.

Untitled. 1966–67, after a 1965 original in wood. Painted and burnished aluminum in three identical sections, each 9'3" x 48½" x 24". The Museum of Modern Art, New York. James Thrall Soby Fund. *Page 108*

Umberto Boccioni
Italian. Born 1882, Reggio Calabria. Died in Verona, 1916.

Unique Forms of Continuity in Space. 1913. Bronze, 43⅞ x 34⅞ x 15¾". The Museum of Modern Art, New York. Acquired through the Lillie P. Bliss Bequest. *Page 49*

Lee Bontecou
American. Born 1931, Providence, Rhode Island. Lives in New York.

Untitled. 1960. Welded metal, canvas, and wire, 55 x 58". Collection Nelson A. Rockefeller, New York. *Page 122*

Émile-Antoine Bourdelle
French. Born 1861, Montauban. To Paris, 1885. Died 1929.

Beethoven, Tragic Mask. 1901. Bronze, 30½" high. The Museum of Modern Art, New York. Grace Rainey Rogers Fund. *Page 36*
Eloquence (Study for the Monument to General Alvear in Buenos Aires). 1917. Plaster, 17⅝" high. Musée Bourdelle, Paris. *Page 38*

Louise Bourgeois
American. Born 1911, Paris. To United States, 1938. Lives in New York.

Quarantania, I. 1948–53. Painted wood, 6'9¼" high, including wood base, 6 x 27¼ x 27". The Museum of Modern Art, New York. Gift of Ruth Stephan Franklin. *Page 96*

Constantin Brancusi
French. Born 1876, Hobitza, Romania. Settled in Paris, 1904. Died 1957.

The Kiss. 1908. Limestone, 23 x 13¾ x 10". The Philadelphia Museum of Art. The Louise and Walter Arensberg Collection. *Page 41*
The New Born. 1916. Marble, 6 x 8⅛ x 5¾". The Philadelphia Museum of Art. The Louise and Walter Arensberg Collection. *Page 22*
Adam and Eve. 1921. Chestnut (one section) and old oak (two sections), 7'4½" high, on limestone base, 5¼" high. The Solomon R. Guggenheim Museum, New York. *Page 56*

Reg Butler (Reginald Cotterell Butler)
British. Born 1913, Buntingford. Lives in Berkhamsted.

The Unknown Political Prisoner (Project for a Monument). 1951–53. Welded bronze and brass wire and sheet, 17⅜" high, on limestone base, 2¾ x 7½ x 7¾". The Museum of Modern Art, New York. Saidie A. May Fund. *Page 124*

Alexander Calder
American. Born 1898, Philadelphia, Pennsylvania. Lives in Roxbury, Connecticut, and Saché, France.

Whale. 1937 (second version, 1964). Stabile: painted sheet steel, 68 x 69½ x 45⅝". The Museum of Modern Art, New York. Gift of the artist (by exchange). *Page 62*
Lobster Trap and Fish Tail. 1939. Mobile: painted steel wire and sheet aluminum, about 8'6" x 9'6". Commissioned for the stairwell of The Museum of Modern Art, New York, by the Advisory Committee. *Page 76*

Anthony Caro
British. Born 1924, London. Taught in United States, 1963–65. Lives in London.

Sculpture Two. 1962. Painted steel, 6'10" x 11'10" x 8'6". Collection Donald Gomme, Compton, Sussex, England. *Page 105*

César (César Baldaccini)
French. Born 1921, Marseilles. Lives in Paris.

Torso. 1954. Welded iron, 30⅜ x 23⅜ x 27⅛". The Museum of Modern Art, New York. Blanchette Rockefeller Fund. *Page 16*

John Chamberlain
American. Born 1927, Rochester, Indiana. Lives in New York.

Untitled. 1960. Welded metal, 20 x 16 x 12". The Joseph H. Hirshhorn Collection, New York. *Page 99*

Pietro Consagra
Italian. Born 1920, Mazara del Vallo, Sicily. Lives in Rome.

Conversation before the Mirror. 1957. Bronze relief, 56 x 40⅞", attached to wood base, 6" high. The Museum of Modern Art, New York. Gift of G. David Thompson. *Page 121*

Hilaire-Germain-Edgar Degas
French. Born 1834, Paris. Died in Paris, 1917.

Dancer Putting on Her Stocking. 1896–1911 (cast 1920). Bronze, 17″ high. The Metropolitan Museum of Art, New York. Bequest of Mrs. H. O. Havemeyer, 1929. The H. O. Havemeyer Collection. *Page 30*

Charles Despiau
French. Born 1874, Mont-de-Marsan. To Paris, 1891. Died 1946.

Assia. 1938. Bronze, 6′3⁄4″ high. The Museum of Modern Art, New York. Gift of Mrs. Simon Guggenheim. *Page 10*

Marcel Duchamp
American. Born 1887, Blainville, France. To United States, 1942. Died in Paris, 1968.

Bottle Rack. 1914. Galvanized iron, 23¼″ high. Photograph of lost original by Man Ray. *Page 52*

Raymond Duchamp-Villon
French. Born 1876, Damville. Died in Cannes, 1918.

The Lovers. 1913. Original plaster relief, 27½ x 46 x 6½″. The Museum of Modern Art, New York. *Page 114*
The Horse. 1914 (first enlargement, cast 1930–31). Bronze, 40 x 39½ x 22⅜″. The Museum of Modern Art, New York. Van Gogh Purchase Fund. *Page 50*

Jacob Epstein
British. Born 1880, New York. To England, 1905. Died in London, 1959.

Oriel Ross. 1932. Bronze, 26¼ x 17″. The Museum of Modern Art, New York. Gift of Edward M. M. Warburg. *Page 28*

Max Ernst
French. Born 1891, Brühl (near Cologne), Germany. To France, 1922; in United States, 1941–50. Lives in Huismes (near Chinon), France.

Lunar Asparagus. 1935. Plaster, 65¼″ high. The Museum of Modern Art, New York. *Page 55*

Henri Étienne-Martin
French. Born 1913, Loriol. Has lived in Paris since 1933.

Demeure 3. 1960 (cast 1965). Bronze (five pieces), 16′4¾″ x 8′2⅜″ x 7′4½″. Collection Michel Couturier, Paris. *Page 90*

Herbert Ferber
American. Born 1906, New York. Lives in New York.

Calligraph with Sloping Roof, One Wall II. 1957–61. Brazed brass, 29 x 39 x 19″. Owned by the artist. *Page 87*

Naum Gabo
American. Born 1890, Briansk, Russia. Worked in Germany, Paris, London; to United States, 1946. Lives in Middlebury, Connecticut.

Column. 1923. Glass, plastic, metal, and wood, 41″ high. The Solomon R. Guggenheim Museum, New York. *Page 66*
Spiral Theme. 1941. Construction in transparent plastic, 5½ x 13¼ x 9⅜″, on two black plastic bases, 16″ square and 23⅞″ square (7½″ high overall). The Museum of Modern Art, New York. Advisory Committee Fund. *Page 67*

Antoni Gaudí
Spanish. Born 1852, Reus. Died in Barcelona, 1926.

Casa Milá ("La Pedrera"), Barcelona. 1905–7. *Page 136*

Alberto Giacometti
Swiss. Born 1901, Stampa. Lived in Paris, 1922–42, 1945–66. Died in Chur, Switzerland, 1966.

The Couple. 1926. Bronze, 23⅝″ high. Kunsthaus, Zurich. Alberto Giacometti Foundation. *Page 54*
The Palace at 4 A.M. 1932–33. Construction in wood, glass, wire, and string, 25 x 28¼ x 15¾″. The Museum of Modern Art, New York. *Page 75*
Cubist Head. 1934–35. Bronze, 7″ high. The Joseph H. Hirshhorn Collection, New York. *Page 24*
Man Pointing. 1947. Bronze, 70½″ high, at base, 12 x 13¼″. The Museum of Modern Art, New York. Gift of Mrs. John D. Rockefeller, 3rd. *Page 11*

Julio González
Spanish. Born 1876, Barcelona. Settled in Paris, 1900. Died in Arcueil, France, 1942.

Woman Combing Her Hair. 1930–33. Iron, 48″ high. Moderna Museet, Stockholm. *Page 74*
Reclining Figure. 1934. Wrought iron, 17¾ x 37″. Collection Nelson A. Rockefeller, New York. *Page 20*
Head. 1935? Wrought iron, 17¾ x 15¼″. The Museum of Modern Art, New York. *Page 24*
Woman Combing Her Hair. 1936. Wrought iron, 52 x 23½ x 24⅝″. The Museum of Modern Art, New York. Mrs. Simon Guggenheim Fund. *Page 83*
The Montserrat. 1936–37. Sheet iron, 65″ high. Stedelijk Museum, Amsterdam. *Page 12*

Raoul Hague
American. Born 1905, Constantinople. To United States, 1921. Has lived in Woodstock, New York, since 1943.

Ohayo Wormy Butternut. 1947–48. Butternut, 66½″ high, attached to base, 3½ x 18 x 11⅞″. The Museum of Modern Art, New York. Katharine Cornell Fund. *Page 17*

David Hare
American. Born 1917, New York. Lives in New York.

Man with Drums. 1947. Bronze, 23″ high. Collection Alice Baber, New York. *Page 54*

Barbara Hepworth
British. Born 1903, Wakefield. Lives in St. Ives.

Head (Elegy). 1952. Mahogany and strings, 7″ high, on base, 1⅜″ high. The Joseph H. Hirshhorn Collection, New York. *Page 61*

Jean Ipousteguy
French. Born 1920, Dun-sur-Meuse. Lives in France.

Alexander before Ecbatane. 1965. Bronze, 68″ x about 12′ x 39⅜″. Collection Nelson A. Rockefeller, New York. *Page 111*

Robert Jacobsen
Danish. Born 1912, Copenhagen, Denmark. Has lived in Paris since 1947.

Hengist. 1953. Wrought iron, 30″ high. Musée des Beaux-Arts, Liège. *Page 71*

Donald Judd
American. Born 1928, Excelsior, Missouri. Lives in New York.

143

Untitled. 1965. Galvanized iron, 11'3″ high (eight boxes: each 9 x 40 x 31″, at 9″ intervals —seven shown in photograph). Gordon Locksley Gallery, Minneapolis. *Page 109*

Gaston Lachaise
American. Born 1882, Paris. To United States, 1906. Died in New York, 1935.

Marianne Moore. 1924 (cast 1946). Bronze, 14⅞ x 8 x 9½″. The Metropolitan Museum of Art, New York. Gift of Lincoln Kirstein, 1959. *Page 27*
Torso. 1930. Bronze, 11½″ high. Whitney Museum of American Art, New York. *Page 16*

Ibram Lassaw
American. Born 1913, Alexandria, Egypt. To United States, 1921. Lives in The Springs, New York.

Kwannon. 1952. Welded bronze with silver, 6' x 43″. The Museum of Modern Art, New York. Katharine Cornell Fund. *Page 79*

Henri Laurens
French. Born 1885, Paris. Died in Paris, 1954.

Head. 1918. Painted wood construction, 20 x 18¼″. The Museum of Modern Art, New York. Van Gogh Purchase Fund. *Page 45*
Crouching Figure. 1940. Bronze, 9 x 11¾″. Musée National d'Art Moderne, Paris. Gift of M and Mme Claude Laurens. *Page 58*

Le Corbusier (Charles-Édouard Jeanneret)
French. Born 1887, La Chaux-de-Fonds, Switzerland. To Paris, 1917. Died in Cap Martin, France, 1965.

Notre Dame du Haut, Ronchamp, France. 1950–54. *Page 138*

Wilhelm Lehmbruck
German. Born 1881, Duisburg-Meiderich. Worked in Paris, Berlin, Zurich. Died in Berlin, 1919.

Standing Youth. 1913. Cast stone, 7'8″ high, at base, 36 x 26¾″. The Museum of Modern Art, New York. Gift of Abby Aldrich Rockefeller. *Page 37*

Jacques Lipchitz
American. Born 1891, Druskieniki (then Russia). To Paris, 1909; to United States, 1941. Lives in Hastings-on-Hudson, New York.

Man with a Guitar. 1915. Stone, 38¼″ high, at base, 7¾″ square. The Museum of Modern Art, New York. Mrs. Simon Guggenheim Fund (by exchange). *Page 44*
Reclining Nude with Guitar. 1928. Black limestone, 16⅜″ high, at base, 27⅝ x 13½″. The Museum of Modern Art, New York. Promised gift and extended loan from Mrs. John D. Rockefeller, 3rd. *Page 21*
Song of the Vowels. 1931–32. Bronze, 10' high. Kunsthaus, Zurich. *Page 57*

Richard Lippold
American. Born 1915, Milwaukee, Wisconsin. To New York, 1944. Lives in Locust Valley, New York.

Variation Number 7: Full Moon. 1949–50. Brass rods and nickel-chromium and stainless steel wire, 10 x 6'. The Museum of Modern Art, New York. Mrs. Simon Guggenheim Fund. *Page 78*

Seymour Lipton
American. Born 1903, New York. Lives in New York.

Sea King. 1956. Nickel-silver on monelmetal, 30½ x 41¾ x 20″. Albright-Knox Art Gallery, Buffalo. *Page 85*

Victor A. Lundy
American. Born 1923, New York. Lives in New York.

Inflatable Exhibition Building for the Atomic Energy Commission. 1960–63. Birdair Structures, Inc. *Page 140*

Aristide Maillol
French. Born 1861, Banyuls. Lived in Marly-le-Roi (near Paris) and Banyuls. Died in Banyuls, 1944.

The Mediterranean. 1902–5. Bronze, 41″ high, at base, 45 x 29¾″. The Museum of Modern Art, New York. Gift of Stephen C. Clark. *Page 39*
Desire. 1906–8. Tinted plaster relief, 46⅞ x 45″. The Museum of Modern Art, New York. Gift of the artist. *Page 115*
Ile de France (Torso). ca. 1910. Bronze, 43″ high. The Metropolitan Museum of Art, New York. Purchase, Edith Chapman Fund, 1951, from The Museum of Modern Art, New York, gift of A. Conger Goodyear. *Page 15*

Robert Mallary
American. Born 1917, Toledo, Ohio. Lives in New Rochelle, New York.

In Flight. 1957. Relief of wood, dust, sand, synthetic polymer resin on painted plywood, 43½″ x 6'7⅝″ x 4⅜″. The Museum of Modern Art, New York. Larry Aldrich Foundation Fund. *Page 123*

Marino Marini
Italian. Born 1901, Pistoia. Has lived in Milan since 1940.

Curt Valentin. 1953. Bronze, 9½″ high. The Joseph H. Hirshhorn Collection, New York. *Page 29*

Henri Matisse
French. Born 1869, Le Cateau. Lived in Paris and Nice. Died in Nice, 1954.

Reclining Nude, I. 1907. Bronze, 13½ x 19¾″. The Museum of Modern Art, New York. Acquired through the Lillie P. Bliss Bequest. *Page 18*
The Back, IV. 1929? Bronze, 6'2″ x 44¼″ x 6″. The Museum of Modern Art, New York. Mrs. Simon Guggenheim Fund. *Page 116*
Tiari. 1930. Bronze, 8″ high. The Museum of Modern Art, New York. A Conger Goodyear Fund. *Page 23*

Kasimir Meduniezky
Russian. Born ca. 1899.

Construction Number 557. 1919. Tin, brass, and iron, 17¾″ high including base. Yale University Art Gallery. Collection Société Anonyme, bequest of Katherine S. Dreier. *Page 65*

Eric Mendelsohn
British. Born 1887, Allenstein, East Prussia. Worked in England and Palestine, 1933–41; to United States, 1941. Died in San Francisco, 1953.

Einstein Tower, Potsdam, Germany. 1920–21. *Page 137*

Joan Miró
Spanish. Born 1893, Montroig (near Barcelona). In Paris, 1914–40. Has lived in Palma de Mallorca since 1956.

Poetic Object. 1936. Assemblage: stuffed parrot on wood perch, stuffed silk stocking with velvet garter and doll's paper shoe suspended

on a hollow wood frame, derby hat, hanging cork ball, celluloid fish, and engraved map, 31⅞ x 11⅞ x 10¼". The Museum of Modern Art, New York. Gift of Mr. and Mrs. Pierre Matisse. *Page 95*

László Moholy-Nagy
American. Born 1895, Bacsbarsod, Hungary. In Berlin, 1920–34; to United States, 1937. Died in Chicago, 1946.

Space Modulator. 1940. Plexiglass and wire, 20" high, mounted on stainless steel plate, 28 x 18". Formerly Collection Mrs. Sibyl Moholy-Nagy, New York (accidentally destroyed). *Page 68*

Henry Moore
British. Born 1898, Castleford. Lives in Much Hadham.

Reclining Woman. 1930. Green Hornton stone, 36" long. The National Gallery of Canada, Ottawa. *Page 19*
Two Forms. 1934. Pynkado wood, 11 x 17¾", on irregular oak base, 21 x 12½". The Museum of Modern Art, New York. Sir Michael Sadler Fund. *Page 60*
King and Queen. 1952–53. Bronze, 64½" high. Collection W. J. Keswick, Scotland. *Page 126*

Robert Müller
Swiss. Born 1920, Zurich. To Paris, 1949. Lives in Villiers-le-Bel (near Paris).

Aaron's Rod. 1958. Welded metal, 66" high. Galerie Beyeler, Basel. *Page 86*

Reuben Nakian
American. Born 1897, College Point, New York. Has lived in Stamford, Connecticut, since 1944.

Olympia. 1961. Bronze, 6 x 6 x 6'. Whitney Museum of American Art, New York. Gift of the Friends of the Whitney. *Page 88*

Louise Nevelson
American. Born 1900, Kiev, Russia. To United States, 1905. Lives in New York.

Sky Cathedral. 1958. Assemblage: wood construction painted black, 11'3½" x 10'¼" x 1'6". The Museum of Modern Art, New York. Gift of Mr. and Mrs. Ben Mildwoff. *Page 119*

Ben Nicholson
British. Born 1894, Denham. Has lived in Tessin, Switzerland, since 1958.

Painted Relief. 1939. Synthetic board mounted on plywood, painted, 32⅞ x 45". The Museum of Modern Art, New York. Gift of H. S. Ede and the artist (by exchange). *Page 118*

Constantino Nivola
Italian. Born 1911, Orani, Sardinia. To United States, 1939. Has lived in The Springs, New York, since 1949.

Freestanding Mural. 1964. Cement cast on sand mold, 8' high. Recreation Area, Stephen Wise Towers, New York City Housing Authority. *Page 120*

Isamu Noguchi
American. Born 1904, Los Angeles, California. In Japan, 1906–18. Has worked in United States, Paris, Peking, Japan. Lives in Long Island City, New York.

Sunken Courtyard. 1960–64. Beinecke Rare Book and Manuscript Library, Yale University, New Haven. *Page 130*

Claes Oldenburg
American. Born 1929, Stockholm, Sweden. Settled in United States, 1936. Lives in New York.

Giant Soft Fan. 1966–67. Vinyl, wood, and foam rubber, 10' x 59" x 64"; cord and plug, 24'3¼". The Museum of Modern Art, New York. The Sidney and Harriet Janis Collection. *Page 112*

Eduardo Paolozzi
British. Born 1924, Edinburgh, Scotland. Lives in London.

Hermaphroditic Idol Number 1. 1962. Aluminum, 70½ x 27½ x 22". Museu de Arte Contemporânea da Universidade de São Paulo. *Page 113*

Antoine Pevsner
French. Born 1886, Orel, Russia. Settled in Paris, 1923. Died 1962.

Developable Column. 1942. Brass and oxidized bronze, 20¾" high, on base, 19⅜" diameter. The Museum of Modern Art, New York. *Page 70*
Bird Flight. 1955–56. Bronze, 16' high, on Swedish red granite base, 48 x 40 x 52". General Motors, Warren, Michigan. *Page 128*

Pablo Picasso
Spanish. Born 1881, Malaga. To Paris, 1900. Lives in Mougins, France.

Woman's Head. 1909. Bronze, 16¼" high. The Museum of Modern Art, New York. *Page 42*
Still Life. 1914. Painted wood with upholstery fringe, 10⅛ x 18 x 4". The Tate Gallery, London. *Page 93*
Construction in Wire. 1928–29. Iron wire, 19¾ x 16⅛ x 6¾". Owned by the artist. *Page 73*
Bull's Head. 1943. Bronze, after bicycle seat and handlebars, 16⅜ x 16½ x 6". Owned by the artist. *Page 53*
Death's Head (Flayed Head). 1944. Bronze, 11⅜ x 8⅜ x 10¼". Owned by the artist. *Page 25*
Man with Sheep. 1944. Bronze, 6'8" x 30½" x 31". Owned by the artist. *Page 13*
The Bathers. 1956. Bronze, after wood. Six figures: bather, 8'8" x 33⅜"; man with joined hands, 8¾" x 32½"; fountain man, 7'¼" x 25⅝"; diver, 6'6½" x 69"; bather, 69¾ x 19½"; head 53½ x 27". Collection Nelson A. Rockefeller, New York. *Page 129*

George Rickey
American. Born 1907, South Bend, Indiana. In Scotland, 1913–30; in New York 1934–37. Lives in East Chatham, New York.

Two Lines—Temporal I. 1964. Two stainless steel mobile blades on painted steel base, 35'2¾" high (overall). The Museum of Modern Art, New York. Mrs. Simon Guggenheim Fund. *Page 104*

Gerrit Thomas Rietveld
Dutch. Born 1888, Utrecht. Died in Utrecht, 1964.
Schröder House, Utrecht, the Netherlands. 1924. *Page 134*

José de Rivera
American. Born 1904, West Baton Rouge, Louisiana. Lives in New York.

Construction 8. 1954. Forged stainless steel, 9⅜" high. The Museum of Modern Art, New York. Gift of Mrs. Heinz Schultz in memory of her husband. *Page 81*

Auguste Rodin
French. Born 1840, Paris. Moved to Meudon (near Paris), 1894. Died 1917.

The Walking Man. 1877–78 (cast before 1908). Bronze, 33¾" high (original scale). Collection Edward Steichen, West Redding, Connecticut. *Page 14*

Model for a Monument to Labor. 1894. Plaster, 36″ high. Musée Rodin, Meudon. *Page 132*

Monument to Balzac. 1897 (cast 1954). Bronze, 9′3″ high, at base, 48½ x 41″. The Museum of Modern Art, New York. Presented in memory of Curt Valentin by his friends. *Page 35*

Baudelaire. 1898. Bronze, 8″ high. Collection Arthur Strilky, Chicago. *Page 26*

Dance Movement D. 1911 (cast 1946). Bronze, 13″ high. Collection Mrs. Samuel Bronfman, Montreal. *Page 32*

Medardo Rosso
Italian. Born 1858, Turin. Lived in Paris, 1889–1917. Died in Milan, 1928.

The Bookmaker. 1894. Wax over plaster, 17½ x 13 x 14″ (irregular). The Museum of Modern Art, New York. Acquired through the Lillie P. Bliss Bequest. *Page 31*

Eero Saarinen
American. Born 1910, Kirkkonummi, Finland. To United States, 1923. Died in Ann Arbor, Michigan, 1961.

TWA Terminal, Kennedy International Airport, New York. 1957–62. *Page 139*

Kurt Schwitters
British. Born 1887, Hanover, Germany. To England 1940. Died in Ambleside, 1948.

Merz Construction. 1921. Painted wood, wire, and paper, 15 x 8¼ x 2½″. The Philadelphia Museum of Art. A. E. Gallatin Collection. *Page 94*

George Segal
American. Born 1924, New York. Lives in North Brunswick, New Jersey.

Woman Shaving Her Legs. 1963. Plaster, porcelain, shaver, and metal, 63 x 65 x 30″. Collection Mr. and Mrs. Robert B. Mayer, Winnetka, Illinois. *Page 110*

Renée Sintenis
German. Born 1888, Glatz. Died in Berlin, 1965.

Self-Portrait. 1945. Terra cotta, 13⅝″ high, on base, 11″ high. Galerie Alex Vömel, Düsseldorf, Germany. *Page 27*

David Smith
American. Born 1906, Decatur, Indiana. To New York, 1926; to Bolton Landing, New York, 1940. Died 1965.

Hudson River Landscape. 1951. Steel, 6′3″ long. Whitney Museum of American Art, New York. *Page 80*

Tank Totem V. 1955–56. Steel, 12′3¾″ x 52″ x 15″. Collection Mr. and Mrs. Howard Lipman, Cannondale, Connecticut. *Page 84*

Cubi X. 1963. Stainless steel, 10′1⅜″ high. The Museum of Modern Art, New York. *Page 103*

Tony Smith
American. Born 1912, South Orange, New Jersey. Lives in South Orange.

Cigarette. 1967. Cor-ten steel, 15 x 18 x 26′. Albright-Knox Art Gallery, Buffalo. Gift of Seymour H. Knox. *Page 106*

Richard Stankiewicz
American. Born 1922, Philadelphia, Pennsylvania. To New York, 1951. Lives in Huntington, Massachusetts.

Instruction. 1957. Welded scrap iron and steel, 12½ x 13¼ x 6⅛″. The Museum of Modern Art, New York. Philip Johnson Fund. *Page 97*

Mark di Suvero
American. Born 1933, Shanghai, China. To United States, 1941. Lives in New York.

Pre-Columbian. 1965. Wood, steel, rubber, 8′ x 14′ x 10′6″. Storm King Art Center, Mountainville, New York. *Page 98*

Vladimir Tatlin
Russian. Born 1885, Khar'kov or Moscow. Died in Moscow, 1953.

Model for a Monument for the Third International. Original 1920, destroyed. Wood and metal with motor, 15′5″ high. *Page 133*

Jean Tinguely
Swiss. Born 1925, Basel. To Paris, 1951. Lives in Soisy-sur-École (near Paris).

Eureka. 1964. Motorized construction, 30′ high. Collection City of Zurich. *Page 100*

Ossip Zadkine
French. Born 1890, Smolensk, Russia. To Paris, 1909; in United States 1941–45. Died in Paris, 1967.

Mother and Child. 1918. Marble, 23¾″ high. The Joseph H. Hirshhorn Collection, New York. *Page 47*

Selected Bibliography

This selection of recent books on modern sculpture is limited to works of a general nature. Monographs on individual sculptors and books on particular styles or movements are not listed.

Dore Ashton. *Modern American Sculpture.* New York: Harry N. Abrams, 1968.

Alan Bowness. *Modern Sculpture.* New York: Dutton and London: Studio Vista, 1965.

Jack Burnham. *Beyond Modern Sculpture: The Effects of Science and Technology on the Sculpture of this Century.* New York: George Braziller, 1968.

Carola Giedion-Welcker. *Contemporary Sculpture: An Evolution in Volume and Space.* New York: George Wittenborn, 1960.

A. M. Hammacher. *Evolution of Modern Sculpture.* New York: Harry N. Abrams, 1969.

Udo Kulterman. *The New Sculpture: Environments and Assemblages.* New York: Frederick A. Praeger, 1968.

Fred Licht. *Sculpture: 19th & 20th Centuries.* Greenwich, Conn.: New York Graphic Society, 1967.

Herbert Read. *A Concise History of Modern Sculpture.* New York: Frederick A. Praeger, 1964.

George Rickey. *Constructivism: Origins and Evolution.* New York: George Braziller, 1967.

Andrew Carnduff Ritchie. *Sculpture of the Twentieth Century.* New York: The Museum of Modern Art, 1952.

Jean Selz. *Modern Sculpture: Origins and Evolution.* New York: George Braziller, 1963.

Michel Seuphor. *The Sculpture of this Century.* New York: George Braziller, 1960.

Eduard Trier. *Form and Space: Sculpture of the Twentieth Century.* New York: Frederick A. Praeger, 1962; revised, 1968.

Maurice Tuchman. *American Sculpture of the Sixties.* Greenwich, Conn.: New York Graphic Society, 1967.